CW01511852

Remembering
the Ancestral Soul:
Soul Loss and Recovery

by

Jane Ely, Ph.D., D.Min.

authorHOUSE™

1663 LIBERTY DRIVE, SUITE 200
BLOOMINGTON, INDIANA 47403
(800) 839-8640
WWW.AUTHORHOUSE.COM

First published by AuthorHouse 05/11/05

ISBN: 1-4208-3368-5 (sc)

Library of Congress Control Number: 2005901297

Printed in the United States of America
Bloomington, Indiana

This book is printed on acid-free paper.

Cover design by David Nakashita, David Nakashita Communication Design

Grateful acknowledgment is given to the following authors for permission to reprint:

Patricia Reis, The Ancient Ones, Through the Goddess, 1995, Continuum Publishing Company, NYC
Dave Carson and Jim Wilson, Twisted Hair, Tulku Music, 1994
Coleman Barks, God in the Stew, The Glance, Songs of Soul Meeting, 2001, Viking Penquin, NY.
David Whyte, Sweet Darkness, The Journey, The House of Belonging, 1998, Many Rivers Press, Langley, Washington.

And to: D.H. Lawrence, Escape, The Complete Poems of D. H. Lawrence, 1964, Penguin Group, London, UK. Public Domain

Dedication

This work is a poem to all sentient beings and it is dedicated to
The Great Mystery That Moves Through All Things
and to each person, relationship, family, community and, country
who make the choice to engage their full creative capacity and
potential to grow the soul.
It is true, as one grows—so do we all.

Acknowledgments

Simply put, Maura Parks, my mother, and Robert Clooney, friend and colleague, are the midwives of this project. I am profoundly grateful for your dedication and commitment.

I wish to express my deep gratitude and thanksgiving for each one of the Heart Talking Elders. We are so fortunate you are in the world with us, guiding the way.

Kay Cordell Whitaker

Don Alberto Tazto and Silvia Reynoso

Luisah Teish

Patricia Whitebuffalo

Anita Barrows

Matthew Fox

Sandra Ingerman

Arielle Guttman

Sam Beeler

Judith Schmidt

I include with these elders each teacher upon my journey. There have been many, both challenge-teachers and ally-teachers. Grandfather said to me, "I will know how these teachings given to you come through for others because of how you live your life. Live a good life and we will be content and happy." For my teachers then and now, I am truly thankful.

And to each client and student apprentice who has shown me the way as we clasped hands and hearts and "went on the great journey" of soul remembering. It is by the grace of your commitment, integrity, and honesty that our lodge of learning continues.

And last but not least, Anita Barrows, Cristina Gonzalez, and Catherine Vajda, thank you for your blessing ways, your hearts, eyes and expertise.

The Great Medicine Wheel of love continues. We are one.

Table of Contents

Introduction

Part I: Overview

The Ancient Ones

From the beginning,
We have been with you.
We are the ancient ones
And we remember.

We remember the time when there was only love,
The time when all breathing was one.
We remember the seed of your being
Planted in the belly of the vast black night.

We remember the red cave of deep slumber,
The time of forgetting,
The sound of your breath,
The pulse of your heart.
We remember the force
of your longing for life,
The cries of your birth
bringing you forth.
We are the ancient ones
And we have waited
       and watched.
You say you cannot remember that time
That you have no memory of us.
You say you cannot hear our voice
That our touch no longer moves you.
You say there can be no return
That something has been lost,
That there is only
       silence.
We say the time of waiting is over.
We say the silence has been broken.
We say there can be no forgetting now.
We say
      listen
We are the bones of your grandmother's grandmothers.
We have returned now
We say you cannot forget us now
We say we are with you
And you are us.
Remember
      Remember.

(Reis 1995, 36-7)

In the late 1970's I met and became apprenticed to a shaman named Tuguk who taught me about soul loss, the song of the soul, and the remembering process. My first encounter with Tuguk was in Churchill, Manitoba while traveling on business as curator for a Canadian museum. I had installed an exhibition at the Churchill Community Center where Tuguk was visiting to get a diagnosis on an illness. Upon meeting, we became fast friends, both of us sharing a rather offbeat sense of humor. For five years I apprenticed myself to Tuguk until he crossed through the veil and went back to the lands of his ancestors. It was during this time of apprenticeship that I learned about shamanism and spiritual practice according to his world and life experiences. Tuguk first introduced me to trance journeying through a technique he called "gazing." And, in learning how to gaze, I began to see in other realities just as I had as a child. I remembered how to see, which in itself was a soul retrieval. Later during my apprenticeship, Tuguk taught me about soul remembering that has become a lifelong spiritual practice.

Soul remembering has aided and supported me during times of tremendous loss, illness, death, accidents, depression and divorce. As a healing practice and as a spiritual practice, the work of recovering lost fragments of myself during trauma, shock and grief has been a steadying force of healing in my life. As a result of the healing I experienced with this spiritual practice, I became so passionate about the process of soul recovery that I began to look into other indigenous cultures' spiritual ways of balancing and harmonizing. This search opened the doors to many other spiritual and healing traditions that I have studied for years.

From the time of that initial teaching on soul retrieval from Tuguk, I began to seek out and study other healing ways. I made a commitment to walk the medicine way of my indigenous elders and teachers, and it changed the course of my life. It was not until I began to study other healing traditions that I realized how prevalent the concept of soul loss and recovery is in indigenous cultures that have maintained the integrity of their shamanic traditions.

The premise of the book is to explore a powerful indigenous healing way, to apply it to our post-modern present condition, and to examine the validity of soul remembering as a healing method.

In this book, *Remembering the Ancestral Soul: Soul Loss and Recovery*, I honor the ancestors who practice and preserve healing ways (see Introduction – Part II). I explore the principles of Creation Spirituality and The Medicine Wheel of Life that I have been taught as it relates to the healing process of soul loss (dismemberment) and the journey around the circle to soul recovery (remembering). Healing is not a linear process, as I experience it, nor does it occur in an orderly step-by-step fashion around the circle. I personally have been practicing soul recovery most of my life. The life journey of remembering has become my spiritual practice.

In Chapter One I delve deeply into the research of ethnography, medical anthropology, and shamanism. I chose to explore cross-cultural traditions in my curiosity about soul loss and recovery as a healing way. Examples and descriptions of indigenous cultures that have preserved the ancestral ways of shamanic healing comprise the major portion of the chapter. Also, indigenous cultures that do not share the practice are discussed. The chapter is a review of knowledge gathered by ethnographers and anthropologists in the field. I write about my experience in a soul retrieval healing I received while in Ecuador in March, 2001. Included in Chapter One are the causes, symptoms, diagnoses, healing rites and treatment methods of soul loss as practiced by indigenous peoples.

Chapter Two delves into the question of the epidemic of soul loss in our world. It explores the concept of soul loss and soul recovery from the individual perspective into a larger global context. I look at topics such as polluting the earth as an act of soul loss not only for the human species but also for all sentient life and our Mother, the Earth. An underlying theme was to bring soul remembering as a healing methodology into everyday conscious awareness. I feel soul retrieval has major possibilities for our society and our world as a way for the human species to wake-up and stay conscious.

Chapter Three is the heart of the project. Not only did I look to our ancestral knowledge from an indigenous cross-cultural perspective in history, but I also sought out today's medicine men and women—healers, teachers, and therapists to share their wisdom on this topic. Ten elders share their traditions, knowledge, views, and differing perspectives on the epidemic of soul loss and recovery. I share the words of each of these elders in the original interview form so that the voice of the individual can be heard.

Chapter Four explores my own personal experience during healing work. I share a body of personal experience along with my observations of the visual images and impressions I see when doing the "gazing" or soul journeying during healing. I describe the human energy field as I experience it and illustrate the state of being in balance and out of balance. I also explore the causes of soul loss based on issues clients have brought to me during sixteen years in private practice.

Finally, Chapter Five looks at the future for soul remembering as a healing and blessing way relevant to our present situation as individuals and as a world community. Words of wisdom from each elder echo in powerful quotes excerpted from their interviews.

Introduction
Part II

The Use of Conscious Language in the Title
Remembering the Ancestral Soul: Soul Loss and Recovery

The new paradigm of conscious language is one that describes energy within the present NOW context. When consciousness is brought from the past (memory state) and from the future (visioning state) to the present moment, a deep alchemical energy opens within us—one that is empowering, inspiring and nurtures awareness, clarity, and life potential. Words carry powerful healing vibrations of breath and sound, both of which are and have been a means of healing for millennia within indigenous shamanic cultures. One of my elders once told me that the wind was the breath of the earth and that it carried healing energy on its powerful swirling spirals. We are in a specific moment in our history and evolution whereby many of us are consciously bridging the gap between old patterns and the creation of new ones.

Remembering describes the moment of awakening to the desire for wholeness. It lifts memory out of the past and brings it home to the NOW. It is the energy of calling, of weaving threads of consciousness into a personal, present tapestry. Strengthening the soul line is the act of "re-membering," lighting-up filaments of awareness, recalling or re-collecting the mind-full state of true self. The word "remember" derives from the Latin *memor* which means "mindful" and "to bring back" (*New World*, 3rd ed., s.v. "remember"). In the act of remembering is the return from being somehow or in some way separated. Remembering is a powerful healing act. Remembering opens us to our true creative capacity and potential as sentient beings upon this planet and I believe it is a way underneath the radar screen of the "intellect" that opens new neuro-pathways.

The term *Ancestral Soul* represents the lineage holders—the ancestors, those who have come before us (in this case wisdom keepers, elders, teachers) who teach, mark and map our evolution and progression. These Ancient Ones represent the true indigenous nature of our connectedness to all sentient life through the bones and energy of our genetic cellular inheritance. Our cellular inter-being, linked generation-to-generation, is made up of the very elements of the universe. Elements of our home planet (earth, water, wind and fire) and all cellular attributes of ancestral chemistry run through our physical, emotional, mental, and spiritual bodies. All of these elements combine to make up our ancestral tapestry.

The word *Soul* arises from the Germanic and Goth words *saiwala* meaning "belonging to the sea" (ibid., "soul"). The conceptual awareness of the soul arising out of a sea is profound. It leaves one's imagination so open to possibilities—a sea of consciousness; of gradual growth and experimentation through millennia of trial and error; literally crawling out of a sea of potential; out of the sea of The Great Mystery That Moves Through All Things. All potentials exist simultaneously; all realities are parallel and interrelated. The soul is unlimited potential. To be inspirited is to be soulful, full of the deepness of belonging, as deep and as mysterious as all the aggregate bodies in the ocean's waters. There is tremendous soul poetry in "belonging to the sea." There is a flow of life, of tides and waves, a greatness that is embodied in all life.

The linking of *Ancestral Soul* merges our history, our cosmological story, our heritage and lineages, interconnected with the sea-of-all-potential. The term I have invented in new paradigm language to describe this awareness is "soulular." It is both the soul remembered and the cells enlivened. To have "soulular" remembrance is to be fully aware, awakened, enlivened and to consciously embody cellular memory and potential of past and future in the present NOW. "Soulular" awareness is both personal and beyond the personal in the larger context of the greater I AM presence; that is, the presence of potential that moves through all things all the time. Becoming and being soulful is the awesome state of being in balance. "Soulular" embodiment is the state of unified habitation in all space and all time. There is no separation, no split in consciousness. We are all related, all ways. This is the state of being fully re-membered in the ancestral soul. It is the home run to the NOW.

The second part of the title, *Soul Loss and Recovery,* describes a roadmap for remembering. There is a healing way in many indigenous cultures known as "soul loss and recovery" which will be explored in these pages. It is an energetic spiritual transmission, which incorporates the natural, indigenous, holistic view of utilizing body, mind, emotions and spirit in the reweaving of the soul from states of separation back home into the state of power, balance and unification.

In the text the causes of soul loss from the natural unified state of harmony to being frayed or afraid, split off, and dismembered is explored. The healing way of re-collecting the fragments of the soul that have split during times of loss are essential to bring back in order to grow the soul. The state of being dispirited and the act of recovery to the state of becoming "inspired" or "in-spirited" is the process of re-collecting the lost fragments.

Life is an organic process. The cycle we are attuned to is one of birth, life, death, rebirth. There are unseen cycles in the realms of the spirit world—the world of faith, trust, mystery, and prophecy. These states of other realities and other dimensions are the landscape of the soul—the unthought, unknown that is also paradoxically the homeland and the foundation of hope, trust, truth, awe and wonder. The energetics of the soul carry life lessons, the blueprint or roadmap of potential individual life choices and challenges interwoven with the oversoul (or the divine infinite, unending soul) that is part of all life. Certain life experiences and ways in which the soul of the individual progresses contributes to soul loss or soul growth. Soul growth is the healing way of recovering that that has been lost back home to the present moment. "Soulular" remembering plants seeds for evolution.

Creation Spirituality, The Medicine Wheel, and Soul Loss and Recovery

Remembering the Ancestral Soul: Soul Loss and Recovery describes a life process that is at once spiritual, physical, emotional and intellectual, historical and cosmological. Our true inheritance is wholeness, oneness and unity. Soul recovery is the process, in Creation Spirituality terms, of moving through the Medicine Wheel of life or the full progression from soul loss to remembering. The *via positiva* from the Creation Spirituality perspective is grounded in birthright--gifts and talents, earthy nature which then moves organically into the *via negativa*, the dark night of the soul, soul loss and forgetting. Arising through the maturation process through conscious choice, self-responsible behavior and action into the *via transformativa*, transforming or growing the soul through the work of being a change maker, utilizing the strength of awe, wonder and the spiritual dimensions to create and effect change. Out of the *via transformativa* is re-birthed the fiery essence of *via creativa*—the path of impassioned radical living and loving. *Via creativa,* living in and from the creative heart is the opportunity for bridging the worlds. It is the "yes-ness" of illumination, joy, and openness—a clear sky, the soul living its potential.

The Medicine Wheel of the four directions (i.e., minimum four directions; there are more in indigenous teachings) that I was taught closely relates to Creation Spirituality. The Southern Direction which is the home of trust, love, innocence and wonder in the Medicine Wheel tradition compares to the *via positiva* in the Creation Spirituality model. Its element is earth, mother, home, and grounded-ness. It is the childlike (not childish) place of open amazement and of gifts. This is the place of our beginning in wholeness, fullness, and growth. It is the place from where we begin our journey in life beginning by leaving home and traveling the Medicine Wheel. When we walk the path out of the *via positiva*, we carry with us allies and gifts that we will need along the way.

In the Western Direction lies the testing time, the shadow lands, the places of potential, losing track of self and of letting go. The

Western Direction is the home of the *via negativa*, the "challenge-teachers," the "dark night of the soul," or dismemberment. Its element is water and the watery nature of the emotions. Negative behavioral patterns arise continually to reveal life lessons for us to embrace. In delving into the western energies, we face and embrace our greatest fears, the darkest, most ugly part of our beliefs and images about ourselves and our subsequent behaviors. Tremendous gifts are also to be found in our dark nature, but many people never "get" the energetic healing of the west. The tendency is to freeze the western attributes, to resist, get defensive, get lost or ignore these challenge-teachers in our lives. When water freezes, the emotional body gets stuck. So much soul loss happens as the personality aspect of the soul begins to layer illusion over illusion, masking, deflecting, and finally forgetting what it is to fully embody the juicy darkness full of life force. One of the attributes that is essential to cultivate in western direction (*via negativa*) work is the willingness to yield. To yield is to meet what is without embellishment; to sit in discomfort, to grieve, mourn, and feel the loss; and then to become curious about the pain. Exploring pain and the nature of suffering is very much part of western direction work. It is the beginning of thawing and of recalling the soul. Many people never explore and mine the treasures that are to be found in the darkness; and, thusly, keep returning in repeated recycled behavioral patterns to the challenge-teacher of those life lessons being revealed in the *via negativa*. A pattern of repeated disempowerment or leaky self-neglect causes soul loss. Suffering either grows the soul or shrinks the soul. The alleviation of suffering can open the contracted repeating spiral of recycling emotional reactions and responses in a way that strengthens the soul so that it can consciously evolve. Recovering essences of soul fragments or parts that have split off "re-unites" the soul. The song of the soul begins to hum and get stronger. The soul literally is remembering itself—singing itself home out of the darkness and, in singing, the soul becomes bright.

The Northern Direction is the home of our wisdom teachers, elders, and ancestors. It is the energy and nature of our allies, our support. In the Medicine Wheel we rely upon the wisdom of our elders to remind us of serenity and the peaceful attributes that grow within us as we learn to reference and touch into our inner depths. We learn to lean into the inner landscape of self-responsible wisdom, the voice of discernment and truth that guides us. The element of air clears away confusion and blows fresh wind into the mind, reminding and refreshing it. In Creation Spirituality the northern direction parallel would be the *via transformativa*, the place of compassion, maturation, inner confidence, and taking right action (or justice-making). In the spiritual way of soul recovery, this healing is the act of integrating the soul's return into the emotional and mental consciousnesses and the cellular physical body. The process of reweaving the soul continues in the *via transformativa* as the filaments of remembering inhabit the NOW with more and more vibrational frequency. Integration is the act of re-embodying the soul song and of filling up. A "transformer" in the English language can also mean a conductor of energy (current or voltage). The *via transformativa* aspect of soul reweaving increases the current of life force and turns up the volume of the soul song so that the tune and words are clearly audible.

The *via creativa* in Creation Spirituality is parallel to the Eastern Direction in the Medicine Wheel. This direction is the home of fire and vision. It is the place where compassion marries passion in the awesome current of creative awareness and manifestation. Fire fuels the joy of the soul returning and reweaves it into balance. It is like the call of a bonfire burning in an open field as you pick your way through a forest in the darkness on the way home. You can see the fire from a long distance away. It lights your heart with hope and knowledge that you are on the right path. It beckons and calls. Fire helps us remember home, hearth, warmth, comfort, joy and natural balance. Fire illuminates the path home and supports us in visioning—by firing the imagination from within. Fire also burns the dross of old behavioral patterns that no longer serve us. Utilizing creativity for remembering the soul, lighting the way, igniting the imagination and manifesting spirit is part of integration and the completion of the circle of soul recovery. Living fully embodied from the heart of creativity is our natural state of being connected to all life.

The elements of the Sun and Moon, the Sky and Star Nations surround and support us in the Upper World of the Cosmos. The Great Mystery in the Medicine Wheel interacts with all life. The Mother Earth at the center of the wheel supports the Tree of Life, the manifestation of life in the form of the third dimension of the physical world that also grows at the center of the spirit world. The

Tree of Life stands in the Center of the Medicine Wheel connecting this world to other spiritual realities.

The model of Creation Spirituality has parallel and sometimes similar attributes to the Medicine Wheel and to the healing ceremony of soul remembering. [Note to reader: In comparing, be careful not to layer one system over another to force a fit. There are enough echoes between these ways that inform and delight us. Each way, however, has differences and depths not covered here.] A circle's energy, as in the Medicine Wheel or Creation Spirituality model, is vastly different from linear Westernized black and white compartmentalized linear energy. Circular thought, for example, encompasses all aspects of life in unity, without split or separation. The circle of soul loss and recovery is a whole way of being. In the circle of unification, we are never really lost. We are "dismembered" but not gone. When the transmissional energy of remembering and "in-spiriting" is brought into play with the dismembered fragment or filament of the soul, it rewires and ignites the light of the soul. The strength and brightness of the fire of the already burning soul can be active, vibrant, and vitally alive; or, in the struggling soul, weakening, dim, or about to go out. The transmissional healing of soul-remembering rekindles the soul, adding more fuel to the fire essence. The fire of the divine soul can never truly go out for it is the soul part of us that is infinite. The physical life force does, however, die. At death the soul transforms through the physical, emotional, and mental realms of the third dimension to incorporate with the divine soul. The divine soul in anthropological studies is known as the "free-soul" (Hultkrantz 1953, 27).

Chapter 1

Soul Loss and Recovery as a Spiritual Healing Method in Indigenous Cultures: A Historical Review from Medical Anthropology, Ethnology, and Shamanic Perspectives

Twisted Hair

This was the way of it,
let the story fires be lighted
let our circle be strong and full of medicine
Hear me this is my dream song, that I am singing for you
This is my power song that is taking me to the edge
This is my talking birth song for a new day
This is rock medicine, the talking tree, the singing water

Listen…I am dancing underneath you.

It is a memory, a river, it is a chant
it is a memory of long ago
it is an arrow in flight, a medicine story
it is what happened long ago
it is a bead in a story belt
it is what has been forgotten
it is a campfire, the smell of sweet grass and cedar
prayers lifted to sky father, tradition, the way it was always done by
the people
the feeling of warmth and the sound of voices

Listen I am dancing underneath you

I am dancing on the shore of a river, in the moonlight
calling you to the campfire
to sit with the people and remember

listen I am dancing underneath you

(Song by Dave Carson and Jim Wilson, www.TulkuMusic.com, 1994)

Soul Loss and Recovery

Historical references in the state known as soul loss appear in many ethnographic texts, in studies of medical anthropology, and in works written on shamanism. The topic is big and well recorded and yet, in present day conscious memory, all but forgotten and certainly not shared openly when discussion arises in indigenous cultural circles. Indigenous beliefs differ and vary greatly from tribe to tribe. To date, from review and personal experience, it appears that a majority of indigenous cultures have practiced or still are practicing soul recovery in various healing forms in the lands we now know as North American, Central America, South America, Northern Siberia, Mongolia, Indonesia, the Aborigines of Australia and parts of Africa, to name only some of the broad hemispheric regions. Of course not all tribes practice in the same way nor do all tribal ways even consider soul loss a definitive state. Cultural language and perspective differ when describing spirit sickness versus actual soul loss. Suffice to say, soul loss and the practice of remembering and recovery is a shared and prevalent spiritual belief and is an important healing practice in many indigenous world cultures.

> A society's medicine consists in those cultural practices, methods, techniques, and substances, embedded in a matrix of values, traditions, beliefs, and patterns of ecological adaptation, that provide the means for maintaining health and preventing or ameliorating disease and injury in its members (Landy 1977, 31).

> The old man explained that in the trance vision one can see a 'web of intersecting threads' on which the scenes of the tangible world as well as dreams and visions are hung. 'Inner fears,' he said, 'break that glimpse of an invisible web cord, leaving only

3

a world of isolated things…Anyone who does not know how to find food and feed himself is always frightened inside…and with that fear the vision of the spirit world departs' (Lawlor 1991, 373).

The soul is described in the ethnographic research of Ake Hultkrantz in *Conceptions of the Soul Among North American Indians* (1953), a study in religious ethnology. Dr. Hultkrantz did direct field research in the 1940's and 50's, living and working within Native American cultures, primarily concentrating on the Plains and Great Plains tribes, and the Ojibway of the Great Lakes, the Stoneys of the Alberta Rockies, the Wind Shoshoni, Chumash of southern California, West Coast Salish, and the Zuni of New Mexico, to name a few. He is a champion of indigenous beliefs and culture and has written clearly on the very complex concept of the soul and the psycho-spiritual rites of healing of soul recovery (among many other healing rites).

Hultkrantz's years of investigation describe characteristics of the soul in unitive, dualistic and multi-soul concepts (Hultkrantz 1953, 18-36). The belief is that the soul is multi-faceted, having consciousness and awareness on many levels such as in the spirit realms, and the physical and emotional realms. "The characteristic feature of dualism of the soul lies in the fact that the body-soul manifests the life of the waking individual, whereas the free-soul is the spiritual principle which is active while the body is in a passive state…For when the body is sleeping the free-soul has more or less completely taken over the role of the ego-soul. It is sometimes in the shape of the free-soul that the sleeping individual has his dream-experiences" (ibid., 27). The concept of multilevels of consciousness of the soul is evident also in Australian Aboriginal beliefs such as the totemic soul, relating to sources of life, soul essence, the spiritual and physical make-up of a person; the ancestral soul relating to the Creative Ancestors of the Dreamtime, the realm of archetypal and familial lineage holders; and the ego-soul relating to the individual's life and relationships, also known as the Trickster (Lawlor 1991, 345).

Mircea Eliade describes the indigenous peoples of Indonesia and Central and North Asia beliefs as the soul having three to seven multiple principles. "One part of the soul is the individual and dies at death, another part goes to the realm of the shades (shadowland or land of the ancestors) and a third part ascends to the sky and is eternal" (Eliade 1964, 216).

In Mongolian beliefs the human being has three soul aspects: the *suld, ami* and *suns* souls. Throughout Siberia and Mongolia, it is common knowledge that humans and animals need multiple souls to keep the physical body alive. The Samoyed believe women have four and men have five soul aspects, but most Siberians believe that there are three souls. The suld resides in the crown charka and is necessary for the body to live. It is connected to the eternal Father Heaven. After death it goes to reside in nature. It has no past life experiences and does not reincarnate (Sarangerel 2000, 50).

The ami soul enlivens the body, also known as the breath soul. Ami reincarnates and carries ancestral lineage, wisdom and genetic memory. Ami can get displaced during spirit illness or soul loss. The suns soul carries with it the collective experiences of past lives and is part of the personality. Ami and suns must live in balance and harmony but can be dislocated or dismembered for some periods of time and then recovered to health and balance. But if the suld soul is lost, death will almost always follow (ibid., 51-56)

Inuit hold the belief that there is one soul with several distinct component parts. The Inuit names for these two aspects are breath-soul and shadow-soul. Breath is life-force, warmth, the enlivened body, consciousness, will, reason, the person. The shadow aspect of the soul is the free-soul, the aspect that lives, travels and is the dreaming, ecstatic nature of soul. Inuit describe the breath-soul as *inusia,* "one with the spirit of life." (Rasmussen 1919:23). Breath is the animating aspect of soul found over and over again in indigenous cultures relating to inter-being with all life forces. As we explore other attributes of soul characteristics, breath and sound, particularly the soul song, become very important in the animation and healing of the soul.

> *Susto* or soul loss is a prevalent condition in indigenous and Hispanic-speaking Americans from Central America throughout South America. Indigenous and non-indigenous, male and female, rich and poor, rural and urban peoples of these regions have been recorded as holding the belief of soul loss as well as in the United States in Spanish speaking communities of California, Colorado, New Mexico and Texas (Clark 1959: Saunders). In the aboriginal communities that do not speak Spanish, soul loss is also well known as a healing crisis. (e.g., Chinatec, Tzotzil, Quechua) and in many other cultures consisting of beliefs that an individual is composed of a corporeal being and one or more immaterial souls or spirits which may become detached from the body and wander freely (Landy 1977, 121).

The word *susto* means "a sudden fear" in Spanish. When the word susto is used, it refers to a state of sudden fear that has had a specific effect on an individual.

An important point arises in the research that should be brought out and noted as a difference in beliefs in some indigenous cultures. This is the difference between soul loss and spirit sickness. Spirit sickness is reported mainly in some indigenous cultures with the belief of the existence of a single soul. For example, the Klamath, the Cherokee and the Navajo understand "soul, breath and life" to be expressed as one soul. (Hultkranz 1953, 21). Spirit sickness is a loss of power resulting in physical illnesses that can be and is doctored in healings with herbs or sweat baths for example.

> Soul and mind are almost synonymous to the Cherokee. Our soul has its seat in our heart (my heart: aGi ` na u ´). What we think starts in our heart, and the heart sends our mind out.

> The soul does not leave the body during sleep or dreams. Nor is sickness caused by absence of the soul; but certain psychopathological states are ascribed to this fact; the condition of utter despondency brought about by an enemy 'working' against you is caused by nothing else but the fact that he has gotten hold of your soul, and has buried it 'out west,' in the Night Land (Mooney 1932, 41)

The experiences of soul we are exploring are the soul in multiple aspects. For purposes of clear definition the term "free-soul" will be used to define the part of the soul that leaves the body in states of ecstasy or trance to spiritually and energetically recover the lost (dismembered) soul fragments. The free-soul aspect of the soul is the non-linear, non-physical. It is the aspect of soul that is multidimensional, existing simultaneously within the physical human being but not exclusively. It is spirit, eternal and unending. The free-soul is an aspect of our being which is the mystical aspect, connected to all life, all the time—whether in body but most definitely in spirit. It is the greater I AM, our God presence, The Great Mystery That Moves Through All Things part of us.

Body-soul or ego-soul terms are used to describe the human emotional, physical, intellectual and spiritual conditions that are relational in the third dimension. The body-soul is the aspect of our personality that dies when we leave the corporeal realm. Body-soul or ego-soul are interchangeable terms that describe our material existence. The spiritual aspect of how and in what ways we live our lives is contained also within this way of being. For example, growing the soul through life lessons, meeting and embracing challenges is an essential part of our spirit path. Also, through life experiences how we can lose track of our soul's path such as numbing out or being wounded through trauma (see detailed description of causes and symptoms in Chapter Four entitled, "Soul Loss Now: A Post-Modern Perspective"). All attributes of the free-soul are contained in and are part of the body-soul, (the I AM presence is inter-being). It is only at death or during soul loss (which can lead to death but does not always) that aspects of the soul (whether free-soul or body-soul) disengage from the present. In Kay Cordell Whitaker's interview (see Chapter Three), she discusses this condition as loss of the soul's song. Soul loss is a state of disempowerment caused by fright, trauma or invasion; a state whereby our behavior or outer circumstances acting upon us causes a shock—a rent in the fabric of life-force. The tearing of our webbing can cause spirit sickness (see Sam Beeler and Matt Fox interviews) and soul loss or loss of the soul's song in more extreme cases (see Kay Whitaker, Don Alberto Tazto, Sandra Ingerman, Patricia Whitebuffalo, and Luisah Teish interviews). Soul loss relates and interrelates to the world of nature, this world, and the reality of spirituality and the supernatural worlds (other worldly). The crisis or illness brought on by soul loss relates to all aspects of spiritual and human existence. But not all illness, discomfort or "dis-ease" brings on soul loss. Soul loss can also be caused by a build-up of incremental negative or self-destructive behavior through severe shock(s) or a series of experiences. We must be careful not to lump all challenging life situations into the soul loss category. In Chapter Four, aspects of soul loss are explored relating the condition to our post-modern times; and illustrations of the energy field and the soul line are depicted based on the author's sensory perceptions. First, let us look at causes and symptoms from the perspective of indigenous cultures of our ancestors.

Causes, Symptoms and Diagnoses

When similar causes appear regularly in any specified population and its members respond by manifesting symptoms from which illness or disease eventually arise, a belief or pathology develops. Pathology is the study of the nature and conditions of disease. Indigenous beliefs are circular (holistic), interrelated with the environment, and all life forms including the spirit realms that are integral in maintaining health and balance.

> For the Indians of the Vaupes, S.A. the symbolic importance of rivers…are not just routes of communication, they are the veins of the earth, the link between the living and the dead, the paths along which the ancestors traveled at the beginning of time (Davis 1996, 461).

Being in harmony with the animals and cycles of nature with stages of life growth such as rites of birth, puberty, adulthood, marriage, adopting a relative, eldership and death are all honored in aboriginal cultures. Balance and harmony with the inner landscape of being one with the greater outer environment and The Great Mystery are synonymous. There is no separation in the indigenous mind. What a far cry from the Descartes interpretation of the elements and the earth and all her resources being inanimate objects to be used to support the human species (see Matt Fox interview in Chapter Three). Interconnectedness with rocks, trees, hills, and mountains directly affects the health of the people yet also varies and depends on the cultural context in which each indigenous culture grows. Soul loss interrelates with the environment in which a person grows. What causes shock, sickness or crisis in one person may not affect another deeply enough to cause soul loss. History of shock, woundedness, life experiences, familial background, personality and individual characteristics all affect how, when and in what ways soul loss occurs or not.

Many tribes report soul loss when the human being unwittingly or uncaringly goes out of balance with nature. "The spirits, *manitous,* guard order. They react if humans behave unethically—for instance, if they recklessly kill other people or if they are cruel to animals or kill them wantonly without needing them for food" (Hultkrantz 1992, 29). The reaction of the spirits of nature may be to cause a shortage of food or game, causing mysterious illness that could affect the person. Order and right-way living are normally kept; but when an abhorrent behavior occurs, it is the spirit world that reconciles and brings the person or tribe back into balance. "In all these cases the spirits, manitous, control and supervise infringement of the sacred order and their consequences, the diseases" (ibid., 30). Other causes of illness and soul loss are spiritual intrusions by wizards, witches and persons using medicine in a distorted manner. Magicians in North American tribes have been known in the past to cause suffering, mental disorders, hunger, bad luck, disease and even soul stealing leading to death, if an antidote or counter-medicine is not practiced.

A *midewiwin* (Algonquain medicine man or woman in a society of healers that includes shamans) is called in when soul loss or soul stealing occurs to directly intervene on behalf of the patient. Trained in the spiritual arts, the midewiwin will use one or more methods to heal the loss and/or intrusion. "Curing" is more directed towards a physical disease such as doctoring with herbs, potions, and infusions. Ojibway cultures employ herbalists who are trained in plant medicine, also medicine people who are primarily seers who can diagnose a serious problem. Seeing includes divination by bone reading, trance journeying by the sonic rhythm of drumming or rattling, and accessing the spirits in their non-physical realities to beg and gain their wisdom on the spiritual condition of the patient. These helping spirits open the medicine man or woman's eyes to see in the spirit world. Next, the *jessakid*, Ojibway term for shaman, is called in to hear the diagnosis and to recommend treatment (ibid., 35). (Treatments will be discussed in the next section of this chapter.) The common denominator in all shamanic treatment or doctoring is the ability of the shaman to rely completely and without ego upon the helping spirits. The shaman has aids in the spirit realms upon whom he/she relies as medicine helpers to support and affect change. Soul loss in Ojibway cultures is described thusly:

> ..."the soul that is located in the heart is capable of traveling outside the body, but if it is gone too long, the person will die. Apparently, a short separation of the soul from the body occurs in dreams, while longer absence of the soul due to its ability to return brings disease and ultimate death or in some cases insanity" (ibid., 32).

Symptoms of soul loss include conditions such as drunken-like behavior and actual alcoholism, memory loss, forgetfulness, depression, sudden anger, anxiety, stuttering, disturbed sleep, conflicting desires and behaviors, neurosis, delusions and increasingly illogical, unbalanced behavior patterns.

In Northwest Coast Native American shamanic healing cultures, the medicine man or woman relies upon the helping spirit through merging and becoming one with it. This method is similar to Asian shamanic practice of merging with spirit helpers. Also the medicine spirit merging is found in Iroquois, Tlingit and Haida medicine societies (ibid., 161) who carve elaborate animal masks that incorporate the power and medicine of the spirit helper. The characteristics of medicine are multiple in a mask. For example, a raven with bear ears and human hair, shell eyes, carved from cedar with corn husk adornment will possess and transmit the healing potential of all the spirit elements used in it. Its healing power is animated by the merging of shaman with spirits (ibid., 58).

Other symptoms caused by fright or intrusion include a gradual weakening of the person, withdrawal from daily life—a disempowerment in which the patient begins to fade.

> Power may leave as a result of a psychic shock or activities of the dead. Soul loss also happens when a ghost longs for his "living kin." The theft may be extended over a long time: the dead relative removes piecemeal property belonging to his living kinsman; the loss of a great number of these personal things is the sign that the person has lost his spirit and will die. If, on the other hand, a person is sick without interference from ghosts, but the power is lost according to the diagnosis of the shaman, the destination of the lost power is not necessarily the realm of the dead. The power could linger somewhere in the neighborhood (ibid., 67).

Soul loss is caused by separation brought on by either intentional neglect and actions, unintentional neglect and actions, by an outer fright or inner fear being activated, or by intrusive energies or experiences acting upon a person. South American indigenous (Hispanic speaking, indigenous and non-indigenous nations') causes and symptoms are similar to those of North American tribal cultures.

> Among Indians the soul is believed to be captured because the patient, wittingly or not, has disturbed the spirit guardians of the earth, rivers, ponds, forests, or animals, the soul being held captive until the affront has been expiated. A significant

difference occurs between indigenous and non-indigenous Hispanic speaking peoples. In contrast to indigenous beliefs, soul loss occurs not so much relating to the natural surroundings in contact with nature and the elements but rather by an unexpected accident or encounter that causes shock or fear. Soul loss symptoms, however, are similar: (1) during sleep the patient evidences restlessness; (2) during waking hours patients are characterized by listlessness, loss of appetite, disinterest in dress and personal hygiene, loss of strength, depression and introversion (Landy 1977, 122).

In Muslim Somali, northeast Africa, when soul loss occurs, it is believed another spirit will enter and possess the patient but that possession only takes place in "the absence of the person's own soul…Soul loss sometimes occurs spontaneously in response to a sudden fright or terrifying experience" or aggression. The emphasis on soul loss rather than spirit possession is a strongly developed religious motif in many African societies (Lewis 1971, 48-9).

The Yaruro Indians of Venezuela believe that if the soul is gone long, they are an empty husk and can be possessed by wandering spirits (Lewis 1971, 46). The idea of being emptied during soul loss and, therefore, susceptible to possession by wandering ghosts is frequent in shamanic, indigenous cultures.

In diagnosing patients, the Arctic shaman, according to Mircea Eliade, "is an inspired priest who, in ecstatic trance, ascends to the heavens on 'trips'. In the course of these journeys he persuades or even fights with the gods in order to secure benefits for his fellow men" (Lewis 1971, 49).

I.M. Lewis maintains an integral function of the shaman is to be possessed by spirit (or the helping spirits) during the time of the healing rite. This concept is found in Arctic, North American, Eastern Siberian, Cherokee and Tungus tribes. "The word shaman means literally 'one who is excited, moved or raised,' (and this, incidentally, is very similar to the connotations in other languages employed to describe possession)" (Lewis 1971, 51). Personally, I feel Lewis lumps the art of spirit merging with the supporting guardians in the spirit realms for the purposes of healing in with possession. Possession, in my experience, is entirely different than spirit guardian merging. Possession can happen as a result of soul emptiness whereby a wandering spirit or ghost invades and attaches to a person. Possession is a very complex topic and has many levels of causes.

Another form of soul loss that has been researched in North American tribal cultures is the loss of spirit and power due to the death of a guardian spirit (in non-ordinary reality). Consequences of losing a "lean-upon spirit helper" can cause illness, grief, disempowerment and soul loss in this reality. The guardian spirit "is so intimately connected with the individual that his life is imperiled when the guardian spirit is lost" (Hultkrantz 1953, 370). The guardian spirit has medicine, specific characteristics, supernatural powers and its own guardian or power soul (ibid., 374). These guardians are spirit helpers who are with us all our lives. Some shamans merge with their guardian spirits in doctoring and healing. Amongst the Aboriginal Nation of Australia, the guardian spirit is known as the *familiar* "... a spirit makes an incision in the postulant's abdomen and inserts a spirit-snake, his future 'familiar'." It is common knowledge and practice to go through this rite of passage in Aboriginal culture to receive your guardian spirit; "these powers were not placed at the spiritual pinnacle," but were and are considered as important to life as hunting, dancing, boomerang making, etc. To forget the guardian spirit or familiar is like the death of the soul, a core foundational belief of the Aborigines. When a guardian spirit leaves, it is serious business for the shaman and also for any individual (ibid, 374).

Don Alberto Tazto, Sinchi Yachag, a shaman of the highest order and impeccable training in Ecuador, eloquently describes soul loss in his interview, but it bears insertion here in order to establish the way in which separation happens from the Quechua perspective.

> The loss happens sometimes because of strong fear. Also, you can lose your soul because the path you walk was not in harmony with you. It could also happen because somebody who knows how to make a "work" on you (witchcraft) can steal your soul. It can also be because a person is very weak, maybe you don't have the right way of life, not a good way of life and you can lose your soul. It also happens because the way of living allows another force to come into your body and you lose your soul (Tazto interview, Chapter Three).

Healing Rites of Soul Recovery:
Shamanic Diagnostic Methods

First the symptoms must be correctly recognized as being specific to soul loss. Symptoms that cannot be cured by the normal route of herbal treatments practiced by healers, by prayers and purification, by healing practices such as the Sweat Lodge or other forms of cleansings by medicine men/women are referred to the supernatural healers known as shamans. Shamans work with the spirit world to

16

identify the source of the illness. This process is done in a myriad of spiritual practices all of which require the shaman as a person to remove him/herself from the ego state and to travel to the world of the spirits in a deep trance state. In the spirit world the shaman is shown literal and/or symbolic information that educates the shaman in understanding what needs to be done to bring back the lost soul part. This first step in the soul recovery is a diagnostic trance to check in with the spirits and get confirmation that indeed soul loss has taken place.

Diagnostic methods vary from tribe-to-tribe and culture-to-culture. However, they all have the common practice of forms of divination—i.e., utilizing objects, ceremonies, and trance states to request assistance from the spirit world. Diagnostic rites are extraordinarily important and are carried out in a sacred manner that honors the client, the spirit helpers or spirit guardians of the shaman, the forces of nature, and all the elements of the environment. One thing is clear, it is not the personality of the shaman that is communicating. Communication comes directly through the gateway of trance divination from the spirit world. "The shaman acts as a conduit for the power. He is a mediator between the world of the spirits and the world of men, and it is through him that those in great need of blessing—the sick—receive it" (Lyon 1998, 323). The shaman's talents and gifts are in being impeccable with the chosen method of entering the spirit world, receiving the information, and returning to advise the patient.

Some forms of diagnostic divination require fasting and purification such as vision questing and/or praying in the Sweat

Lodge. These forms of preparation create the ground for the shaman to enter the spirit world with strength, humbleness and clarity. Becoming full or power-full may include singing a medicine song or the shaman's particular soul song that fills him up with spirit and aids him in merging with the spirit world allies in trance states (Hultkrantz 1987, 65).

Songs and chanting are strong forms of medicine. A Netsilik poet [Inuit] described the power of song to Danish explorer Rasmussen in 1931:

> There are so many occasions in one's life when joy or sorrow is felt in such a way that the desire comes to sing…All my being is a song, and I sing as I draw breath…Songs are thoughts, sung out with the breath when people are moved by great forces and ordinary speech no longer suffices…But it will happen that the words we need will come of themselves. When the words we want to use shoot up of themselves—we get a new song (Wilson and Black 1983, 27).

Just one of many examples of the power of song in healing is found in the Navajo tradition, Chantways. Chantways are specific, complex songs and are used for blessing, curing and purification. Blessing Chantways are safeguards for individuals and their material world—i.e., preventive medicine. Curing Chantways are "used to treat illness traced to offenses against various supernaturals and holy people (spirits)…The purification ceremonies known as Evilway or Ghostway chants, purge beings, places and objects of contact with dangerous beings…Evilway rituals are employed to cure the patient" (Lyon 1998, 48-9). Songs and chanting are shamanic diagnostic and healing tools often accompanied by rattling, drumming and dancing which are integral to the song. "As soon as an Indian doctor starts to sing, his power comes close to him and the power is right there with him while he's doctoring" (Hultkrantz 1992, 66).

Other forms of moving into the spirit world for divination and healing purposes are through the use of visionary drugs such as the ritual use of peyote cactus in North America and ayahuasca in South America. Peyote cactus is considered "not a medicine in our sense of the term, but a powerful, supernatural being or thing" (ibid., 94). Peyote is a spirit medicine helper with curative powers which is consumed in a sacred manner in ceremony by the road man (peyote ceremonial leader) and all those seeking healing. The road man who has consumed peyote can look into the patient and see his disease. Peyote is both practiced as a way of diagnosis and also for the patient as a healing medicine (with or without further curing rites in addition to the ceremony).

Richard Evan Schultes, Harvard ethnobotanist, disappeared into the jungles of South American in 1941, and emerged twelve years later with an encyclopedic knowledge and direct experience of hundreds of healing plants. One of those plants, yagé, also known as ayahuasca, was a medicine plant drunk in tea form in ceremonial healing practices. Yagé, used by shamans throughout South America, is considered:

> The source of wisdom itself, the ultimate medium of knowledge for the entire society. To drink yagé is to learn. It is the vehicle by which each person acquires power and direct experience of the divine. The teachers are the yagé people, the elegant beings of the spirit realm, the dwelling place of the shaman grandfathers. Expressing themselves only in song, the yagé people give each

and every Kofan [Kofan is a South American tribe.] has an image, a song, and a vision…No Kofan shares the same motif or the same song. There are as many sacred melodies as there are people, and with the death of a person the song disappears (Davis 1996, 226).

The shaman's duty in taking yagé is to "free his own soul to wander" so that he can identify and diagnose the source of illness. My experience in taking the medicine tea was similar to the description of yagé. In one case a friend had just died, and I knew his soul was confused because he was conflicted in his dying process. When I took the ayahuasca, I consciously began to pray for my friend to go through the veil into the spirit world. I felt my free-soul disengage from my body. My body was singing and dancing in the ceremony but yet a part of me was detached. I began to search for my lost friend's soul, calling out his name. I was soon met by a huge anaconda who took me to where my friend was wandering. He was overjoyed to see me and did not understand that he was dead. We sat down on the ground and I told him; suddenly he smiled and his entire being relaxed. He accepted his death and the anaconda came forward and took his soul into the ancestral spirit lands. I was told not to cross with him but to stay in the realm in which I belonged.

So, in this way, my experience with the medicine power of the tea is in alignment with the literature. It is not a tea to be taken lightly nor out of context for the hallucinogenic effect. In fact, I do not find ayahausca to be a psychotropic drug as it is purported to be. It is a sacred medicinal drink that has strong healing power. And it is taken in a ceremonial way with experienced spiritual elders leading the ceremonies. For me, the tea is like smelling and drinking the sweet nectar of the earth. It is a strong ally in spirit work.

In both the peyote and yagé cultures, the medicine for healing exists and is provided by the plant spirit. Also, the shaman can and does use the altered state supported by the spirit plant in diagnosing soul loss as well as other illnesses. Guardian spirits, spirit helpers, lean-upon animals, and power animals are all terms given to spirit aids in other non-ordinary realities. When the shaman moves into the trance state, it is the spirit helper that reveals the nature of the disease and advises the shaman on a course of action.

> If the condition of the patient indicates that his soul is lost, the medicine man needs the assistance of the guardian spirits to be able to carry through his extra-bodily journey: On his expedition he is accompanied by them as a consequence of the belief he may at times transform himself into their shape. It may happen also, that the shaman refrains from undertaking the journey to the other world and instead sends his guardian spirits after the runaway soul (Hultkrantz 1967, 99).

In a trance state, the shaman can make the transition from the personality state to the ego-less state in the spirit world. The depth of experience in the relationship between the shaman and the spirit guardian is crucial to the task of gathering information and performing healing and often "makes great demands on the psychophysical capacities of the medicine man" (ibid., 99).

The Shaking Tent (also known as the conjuring lodge or the spirit lodge) ceremony (ibid., 1992, 35) ceremony is used by Northern Algonquians and by plateau and prairie-plains tribes of North America as both a means of diagnosis and rescuing a lost soul (ibid., 35). In the Shaking Tent ceremony, the shaman is bound hand and foot, sometimes a blanket is placed over the top and then more ropes are used. The bound shaman is then placed in a darkened tent and the ceremony takes place at night. In the ceremonies I have participated in and witnessed, the shaman is placed in the center of a large darkened meeting room with the tribe and the patient sitting against the walls around the room. As the shaking begins for the shaman, spirit sparks are seen igniting in the room (or coming out the top of the tent). I have also been visited by flying rattles in the dark. The spirit helpers come to advise the shaman. Sometimes the shaman is unbound by the spirits and merges with the spirits to perform healings on people in the room. Sometimes the shaman is consulted by the spirit helpers as to what healing rites the patient needs which is then attended to. In many instances the shaman shifts and is transformed for the duration of the healing into his spirit ally. This shift is known to happen in all indigenous cultures in North, Central and South American (ibid., 1967, 101).

In the Andean (South American) medicine traditions, diagnostic divination is done by a *Yachag* (shaman) through developing clairvoyant perceptions. Disease and soul loss are read in the Quechua culture primarily through fire divination, reading a candle flame passed over the patient; or by a cleansing egg when passed over the person's body reveals illness.

The third form of diagnosis is *cuita fichsha sum,* "sweeping of the guinea pig." The human illness is diagnosed by observing the changes that take place in the animal's body after rubbing it firmly against the patient's body. These divination techniques train the

Yachag to see into the energy field. Soul loss or *susto* is caused by fright, terror or shock. Also *pena*, grief, can cause soul loss. Soul loss is diagnosed by the above methods and is recognized as residing in the liver, which turns white (Rodriguez 1992, 41) according to the Yachag's sight.

There are other indigenous forms of diagnostic methods such as "throwing the bones," the *Yuwipii* (meaning "they bind him" in Lakota) Ceremony similar to the Shaking Tent Ceremony; and the crystal-gazing ceremony that is similar to passing the flame over a person's energy body. The central theme in diagnostic methods is for the shaman to quest power and wisdom from the spirit world through spirit helpers on behalf of a patient while holding a healing intention in an egoless trance state.

Soul Recovery and Healing Rites

Considering healing rites for soul loss depends upon the circumstances and environment; the individual's state of health; self-awareness and personality; and the tribal/cultural belief systems in which the soul loss happened. In shamanic indigenous traditions, these factors are taken into account and are also part of the overall diagnosis and suggested treatment from the spirit world allies. In other words the healing ceremony is specific to the needs of the individual according to the way the soul has separated.

Breath and the use of sucking out intrusions as a result of soul loss and, conversely, as a means of revitalizing the patient and conveying the soul back into the individual is part of the soul recovery process. Along with the use of breath is the use of song to inspire the soul to remember its rightful home. "The shaman's breath is said to have the power to illuminate, which is due to the nature of his heart (called 'breathing thing' in Piman)" (Blackburn 1977, 34).

In soul recovery diagnosis and treatment, there may be direction from the spirits to remove intrusions or energy that has become blocked or stagnant as a result of soul loss. The shaman may need to loosen, expunge, or remove the blockages before actually recovering the soul. "The purpose of sucking must be to remove something and that of blowing, to put something in. If we accept the general equation of life and breath, the meaning of blowing would seem to be to impart life" (ibid., 39).

In some indigenous cultures there is the belief that "bad spirits" (possession) may enter a patient's body as a result of soul loss. Extractions of spirit intrusions and of foreign objects are treated similarly. The shaman, in trance state with the spirit allies, removes or exorcises the intrusive forces (ibid., 1992, 60). An example of soul recovery ceremony in Tlingit and Haida (Northwest Coast) traditional medicine is described:

> There is, finally, the type of spiritual aggression whose result is usually labeled 'soul loss.' In other words, the soul (free-soul) of an individual goes astray or is stolen by spirits, with the consequence that he falls ill…From the data that can be gathered, it seems that the lost or captured soul may lurk in the vicinity or steer its course to the realm of the dead (ibid., 60).

In this case the shaman, after fasting, went out into the woods to catch the lost soul and to entice it to return. Both in Haida and Tlingit cultures a bone or wooden carved instrument known as a "soul- catcher" is used to contain the lost soul. It is recovered and contained in a soul-catcher by the shaman, "the soul was then brought back to the patient and blown into his body" (ibid., 60).

> Medicine men who primarily suck out disease objects (or disease spirits—often spirits turn into objects and vice versa) are to be found almost everywhere (in North America) except in parts of the Southeast and the Southwest...where soul loss and intrusion therapies coexist soul loss curing mostly refers to diseases that affect the individual's consciousness and lead to his slow demise if no cure is set in (therefore the Native words for unconsciousness and death are the same in wide parts of North America). In other places intrusion diseases or soul-loss diseases are dominating disease etiologies, in other words, forming patterns that exclude other types of explanations (ibid., 159).

Wooden or bone "soul-catchers" and crystals (Blackburn 1977, 35) are tools used by shamans to gather. Feathers are used to sweep and cleanse (Hultkrantz 1992, 60).

A specific soul recovery ceremony amongst the Puget Sound tribes of the Northwest Coast known as "The Spirit Canoe" is called for in the case when the lost soul has crossed over to the realm of the dead. Seen as an extreme form of soul loss, a lone shaman's power is not sufficient to call back the forgotten soul. Anthropologist Herman Haeberlin has provided in-depth descriptions of this ceremony (Hultkrantz 1992, 67-70).

In synopsis form, after the diagnosis by the shaman and the guidance given from the spirit allies that the soul is wandering in the land of the dead, a gathering of shamans (at least eight or more) is called. Also, the entire tribe and visiting communities may come to witness this healing. All shamans attending must have the same belief in the realm of the dead, be experienced, and have proven their skills over time. Something along the lines of a major shaman gathering is called in which everyone agrees to cooperate in a spiritual canoeing expedition to recover the lost soul. (In 1978, I participated in a Spirit Canoe ceremony in British Columbia, Canada. Over 500 people came to witness the ceremony and twenty-eight shamans participated.)

It is recommended that visitors to the land of the dead (other than lost souls) travel in a canoe that follows a river into the western direction. The shaman placed themselves in two parallel rows along an east-west axis, facing west. Each shaman is accompanied by an upright board representing the shaman's guardian spirit. In the stern of the human boat stands a shaman who steers the canoe. The patient sits or lies in the middle of the boat. They begin the journey with chanting, singing and drumming, entering into the trance state, crossing the barriers into the spirit world as one large body. The journey continues as they cross over into the land of the dead where shaman(s) seek, find and recover the patient's soul. When this is accomplished, everyone gets up and immediately faces east and paddles swiftly out of the dead realm and back through the spirit world to the shore of this earthly reality. Those holding the soul approach the patient with closed hands and sing the song of the patient's soul back into the body. The ceremony usually takes all night to complete. At the end, the patient rises and the ceremony of soul recovery is complete. Food is then prepared and shared with everyone and a talking council is held in order to recount the epic journey.

In a specific case study offering a testament to the power of this healing, a patient being treated by physicians in hospital for severe neurotic and psychosomatic derangements, and who had made three suicide attempts, was healed. Dr. Jilek, the patient's attending physician supplied a list of other patients who became healthy after this healing ceremony. It is important to note this in light of a medical alternative in situations of psychic or psychosomatic disease (Hultkrantz 1992, 70).

It is reported in many North American tribal soul recovery healing ceremonies that upon return from the spirit world "...the medicine-man blows the soul into the patient's body" (ibid., 1953, 392). The Hopi calls his soul "the breath-body." "The reason for this appears rather natural: a certain materiality must be assumed in the soul if the shaman is to be in a position to catch it and return it to its owner" (ibid.).

The precise location on the body into which the soul is blown varies in tribal practices. Cases describe the area in which there has been disease, the intrusion of which was first extracted, and then the soul recovery journey was performed and the soul was blown directly into that previously afflicted region of the body (Landy 1977, 122). In other beliefs the soul is blown back into the heart region "...the heart, the seat for both soul and power" (Hultkrantz 1953, 401).

In Mongolian shamanic beliefs, there are levels of seriousness in soul loss. If a child's *ami* gets lost (most easy to lose), the child's soul part can be called back by the parents. The *suns* soul is more difficult to call home because it may linger near the body or go to the lower world, a more difficult journey for a shaman to undertake.

When the soul part is found, the shaman places it in his ear or in the drum for the return and then the soul is shaken back into the body of the patient.

The most powerful soul recovery ceremony is known as *dolbor,* or "night road ritual" in Mongolian practice. Beginning at sunset, the shaman goes into the spirit world with the aid of his guardian spirits and follows the World River, called *Dolbor* or *Engedekit* to the entrance of the lower world in the Arctic Ocean. This river is treacherous, full of obstacles and twists and turns. Each shaman lineage has access to the World River through its own tributary. Upon arriving in the lower world, the shaman "may meet Erleg Khan himself, the judge of all souls, and ask for the return of the lost *suns*" (Sarangerel 2000, 103).

Don Alberto Tazto, Sinchi Yachag (senior birdperson or shaman) of the Quechua in Ecuador, describes soul recovery in terms of cleansing rituals first in order to begin the process of harmonizing a person. The use of ritual sour herbs, the egg extraction, and the guinea pig rubbing are all healing methods of removing illness that can cause soul loss. The elements in the shamanic soul recovery ceremony include earth, water, air and fire, and the four directions. The following quote is taken from my journal entry after a healing session with Don Alberto in Ecuador:

> Don Alberto began the ceremony by calling in all the elements of the sacred directions, Pachamama, the earth, the whole planet; Llaukumama, water; Wheydamama, wind; Ninamama, fire; Intipapa, the sun; Kyllamama, the moon; Tchi-tchi, the fifth element which is also called the jushai (the soul of the person being healed). The calling was a beautiful song, turning to face

the directions, and above and below. This harmonized my spirit and prepared the ground for soul reuniting.

Don Alberto continued the healing ceremony by wiping my body with a thick cluster of herbs. Then he used a feather around my energy field and blew herbal water into the afflicted areas of my spirit and body. Finally, he called *shammu, shammu, shammu* which means "come, come, come" to my soul and placed his hands on certain regions of my body, anointing them with a powerful healing oil. "…the Sinchi Yachag must observe…and thus he begins taking out the malaise that the patient says he has. Thus, at the same time that we are diagnosing, we are applying healing" (Rodriguez 1992, 34). The result of the healing is that the four elements are in balance with the fifth element, the *jushai* (the soul). Following the soul retrieval healing, the next day an herbal bath of sweet fragrant flowers and herbs was taken, and specific harmonizing foods were recommended for eating along with rest and being in nature close to the earth and all the elements.

Closing

From indigenous shamanic practices, causes of soul loss and subsequent disease or intrusions arise from fright, shock, terror, anxiety, and accidents; unconscious disconnection from imbalance with nature, the elements, and the environment; abhorrent behavior; loss of a guardian spirit helper; soul stealing by a powerful witch; and ghost sickness; being haunted by the dead. Soul loss may occur in these instances but it also depends upon the individual's state of health, self-awareness, and personality; cultural and societal beliefs;

and the circumstances and environment in which the experience occurred.

Symptoms of soul loss may include changes in behavior and often conflicting behaviors, memory loss, the inability to focus or attend to life, depression, disturbed sleep, more than normal anxiety, gradual weakening of the body or person's attention span, neurosis, delusions and increasingly dissociative behaviors.

Symptoms can be self-diagnosed or diagnosed by close family or tribal members but most often are confirmed by a shaman who performs a diagnostic trance by entering into the spirit world to gain insight and retrieve advice from the helping spirits. The shaman uses tools and aids to get into non-ordinary states of consciousness such as singing, chanting, drumming, rattling, trance dancing and in some cultures medicine plants that alter perceptions and help the shaman to "see" in non-ordinary ways. Also, forms of divination are used such as candle gazing.

It is the guardian spirit helpers that diagnose the illness or the plant spirit helpers that open the shaman's awareness to see, or the shaman's own clairvoyant ability to see into the spirit world.

Healing (soul recovery) rites are specific to the needs advised by the spiritual diagnosis and to the individual. The healing rites also depend upon the patient and the shaman's culture and background. Breath and the use of extracting intrusive objects, blocks or bad spirits through sucking or grabbing and extracting is a common indigenous part of clearing the patient before soul recovery takes place. Many different methods are used in preparation for soul retrieval: cleansing, purification practices, fasting, sweat lodge, cleansing with herbal remedies and diet, cleansing with herbal bouquets and baths, or sweeping with eagle feathers. Breath is also integral to blowing the soul back into the body. Spirit singing and soul songs are also ways of bringing back the soul and "in-spiriting" into the physical realm.

In severe cases of soul loss when the soul has gone to the land of the dead, both the Spirit Canoe Ceremony (Puget Sound and Northwest Coast indigenous practice) and the Night-Road (Mongolian) ceremonies are powerful recovery processes. Supporting the patient to remember balance and harmony in a conscious way of life (spirit, body, mind, and emotions) is the goal of soul recovery. The soul has material presence in our dimension. There is a weight and strength that arises within the individual when recovery takes place and is integrated consciously. We have an increased capacity that opens, a potential or a sense of strength and freedom that is a natural birthright, and our soul line responds accordingly. A sense of spaciousness grows within us, and we feel, sense and act from a deeper ground of confidence.

Chapter 2

The Epidemic of World Soul Loss

Escape

When we get out of the glass bottles of our ego,
and when we escape like squirrels turning in the
cages of our personality
and get into the forests again,
we shall shiver with cold and fright
but things will happen to us
so that we don't know ourselves.

Cool, unlying life will rush in,
and passion will make our bodies taut with power,
we shall stamp our feet with new power
and old things will fall down,
we shall laugh, and institutions will curl up
like
   burnt paper

      Escape, D. H. Lawrence
      (Roberts and Amidon 1991, 101)

The modern age deadened us to matter, teaching as Augustine had sixteen centuries ago that matter and spirit are separate entities. It withdrew soul from animals, plants, mountains, birds, the land, the waters, the forests, and even from the human body from the forehead down. (Our soul is in the pineal gland, said Descartes, eliminating six charkas in the process.) By teaching us that the universe is a machine, other species' bodies are machines, and our bodies are machinelike, modern philosophy took the life out of matter. Inert matter became the object of our senses (Fox 1999, 21).

The primary governing factors in our society are reason, will and emotion. Soul and soulfulness have been assigned to the back pew in institutions with no relevance to the present day of consciousness, nor of interconnection to life. The distortion that rules by reason in our dominant culture is the heavy emphasis on intellectualism. The mind has become the Holy Grail in which all answers to problems are sought. The intellect has "to figure it out" before allowing any movement forward. Interconnected with the mind of reason is will. From a mechanistic perspective, willfulness makes things happen. The use of will in this way creates the illusion of evolution and the illusion of development or movement forward. There are entire countries whose governments operate from the principles of reason and will in the paradigm of making policies and laws from the "power over, greed, and control" perspective. Emotions have been relegated to the basement and are considered negative reactions, hysteria, and oversensitivity. There is no room for the heart and no room for the sacred. Emotions such as grief, sadness, and sorrow are denied, ignored, and squelched. Walking proof can be demonstrated by looking at the massive number of North Americans currently taking doctor-prescribed mood-altering drugs. We are a nation that does not deal well with perceived "negative emotions." In fact, the majority of our responses are fear-based, not love-based. As "we are caught up in the illusions we have created, we are dreaming the wrong dream" (Ingerman 2001, 139).

The disembodiment of the soul from the physical, emotional, and mental aspects of life is profound, the implications of which affect every aspect of life upon this planet. For example, there is no discussion of soul loss in the American medical model. Can you imagine considering your physician as indigenous cultures relate to the shaman or medicine man? Imagine walking into your physician's office, sitting down, and having this conversation:

> You know, doctor, I feel really odd, depressed, anxious, out of sorts. I can't sleep at night and when I do, my dreams are horrible or foreshadow doom or war. My behavior isn't the same. I cancelled my trip that I've been looking forward to because I'm afraid to leave home. I think I may have experienced soul loss as a result of the shock of the September 11 terrorist attacks and the resulting tragedies. I want to cry but I'm all blocked up. Can you diagnose this 'dis-ease' I'm having?

The mechanistic model may treat these symptoms with an antidepressant. Treat the problem not the whole person. Figure out what is wrong (rather than what is right) about the presenting issues. Treat it as a complaint and take steps to stop it from continuing. That type of approach has its source in the reason and will view of life, and it arises out of intellectual defense rather than out of a holistic view (which includes the soul and takes into account so many other spiritual and emotional factors as well). And, lest we not forget, make sure to get the patient out the door within ten to fifteen minutes! Nail the problem and fix it.

This mechanistic model has been increasing in all Euro-influenced cultures the world over. The movement definitely took hold during Descartes' time (1596-1650 AD), but was well underway before his philosophical influence. Religion as institution, authority, intervener, and interpreter had made religion a business under the pretext of saving souls by effectively controlling them. When Euro-cultures arrived in any indigenous society, the mechanistic machine rolled over the "primitives."

> For the Europeans, the true, good, and beautiful human being was a rational individual who could conquer whatever he or she set out to obtain and control. According to this view, anyone who did not seek to conquer was an inferior and weak human being who should be dominated by the 'superior' peoples of the earth. In contrast, the indigenous world of knowledge saw the human as a creature whose very existence depended on interconnectedness within the self, nation, earth, creation, and beyond. (Elizondo 1998, xvii).

The mechanistic model separates, isolates and dominates. On a deep level, the wisdom of the soul's understanding of balance and harmony interconnected with all life has been profoundly compromised. I propose that soul loss exists in countries, nations, and in the majority of humans in the world. Our global policies alone point to the existence of this loss. We are killing the very ground that feeds and sustains us. Our behavior as a species is abhorrent and out of control. Otherwise, how could we kill the very earth that keeps us alive? In indigenous cultures this destructive behavior would signify extreme soul loss. Treating the earth and the elements of nature as inanimate objects is soul killing. "Inanimate literally means 'soulless'" (Fox 1999, 24). Indigenous mind treats the body of the earth as its body—as the circle of all life. Post-modern mind is linear and one pointed with a narrow forward-forcing focus. We have lost basic trust, basic truth, basic balance. We have lost our cosmology, our sense of inter-being. We are in a state of "cosmo-soul loss." A warning from the Cree Nation goes like this:

> Only after the last tree has been cut down,
> Only after the last river has been poisoned,
> Only after the last fish has been caught,
> Only then will you find that money cannot be eaten.
>
> (Fox 1999, 276)

Echoing back to the mechanistic view and practices in the American medical model of today, we find the "out-picturing" of soul loss in the very practice of healing. The Greek physician Asclepius avowed "Do no harm" as the creed upon which today's medical model is based. However, the control-the-symptoms-and-fix-it model has become deeply entrenched. Insurance companies this past year raised rates a minimum of 25%; my insurance broker told me this increase was instituted nationwide. Healthcare is based upon money. There is no spirit in the healthcare business—it is a business, an industry, an institution driven by money.

Thankfully, we live in a country where we have free choice as to how to conduct self-care (which includes spirituality) and preventive medicine. Although, there are ominous rumblings and laws and policies being decided upon that may yet take this freedom of choice away from us. In a recent pamphlet I received announcing a conference on complementary and integrative medicines, the lead message read:

> Complementary and integrative medical therapies are used by an estimated 42% of the U.S. population. Visits to complementary care practitioners exceed visits to primary care physicians by over 200 million visits per year. Americans spend an estimated $30 billion a year on these services, the majority of which is not reimbursed (JAMA 1998, 280:1649-75).

Do you think there would be a conference on complementary and integrative medicine sponsored by Harvard Medical School if the staggering statistics mentioned above did not scare the medical industry to its core? The conclusion I drew from reading between the lines and in reviewing the roster of speakers (all in the medical field) was that this conference was about losing money to traditional healers. Not one traditional healer, not one indigenous healer, not one spiritual leader was invited to speak. The separation of health and soul is profound. And I feel this gap is growing ever wider in the medical institutions out of fear of losing money and control. However, the gap between spirituality and healthcare is closing because more and more people are returning to and seeking out the original healing modalities. People are "voting with their feet" as my grandfather would say. They are turning their attention toward attending to the deeper needs of the overall quality of life which are the true needs of the soul. In this action by 42% of the population (see above quote), there is tremendous power. In this one example of a trend alone, there is soul recovery in massive proportions. The soul's wisdom is seeking balance and harmony that is the natural state of health.

The arising of the soul's wisdom towards balance and harmony must be recovered more consciously. If we are to evolve, we must bring the soul home on massive conscious levels. To accomplish this feat, behavior must change from its leaking, addictive, outer-focused, arrogant, anthropocentric life attitude. In short, we must grow up and become self-responsible. We are eminently capable of doing this. The extent to which we as a species destroy correlates to the extent and power with which we as a species can manifest.

> The day of reckoning has come. In this disintegrating phase of our industrial society, we now see ourselves not as the splendor of creation, but as the most pernicious mode of earthly beings. We are the termination, not the fulfillment of the earth process...We are the violation of earth's most sacred aspects (Berry 1988, 209).

One of the greatest causes of worldwide soul loss within our recorded memory is the advent of nuclear power, nuclear war, and nuclear toxic waste. We are living, for the first time in history, as a human species that holds the power to annihilate itself. The introduction and use of nuclear bombs has fractured a deep life pattern—a sense of organic continuation, or of "going on being" in natural evolutionary growth. The use of nuclear power, "the gourd of ashes" (Suzuki and Knudtson 1993, 241) predicted by the elders of the Hopi Nation, has torn the webbing of life. And so far, we have not found the technology to neutralize the waste. We have created toxic waste that will take 10,000 years to neutralize (according to present scientific speculation). Biological disaster, or "biological severance" as J. Lifton puts it, is a first for us (Macy 1991, 209). Tryone Cashman explains: "When the future is cancelled, there is no need to care for the lands we live on. As former Secretary of Interior James Watt so clearly stated, we can use it all up now because we are the last generation" (ibid, 210).

This truth is buried so deeply in denial that we have largely forgotten it. We have and continue to encourage the nuclear death of all sentient life by burying it. Literally, we are burying toxic waste in the belly of the earth. Ironically, on February 14, 2002 (Valentine's Day), the Bush administration announced plans to bury toxic waste 1,000 feet deep in Yucca Mountain, Nevada. The methods of containing the waste have not been tested. Our technology does not know if the containers will actually withstand 10,000 years. "No containments last as long as the 'poison fire' itself" (Macy 1991, 224). "Scientists speculate that the ground water, another 1,000 feet below the nuclear storage site, will not be affected" (National Public Radio report, February 14 and 15, 2002). Out of sight, out of mind. The entire nuclear threat is buried deeply in denial, yet we condone its continuance.

Somewhere in our psyches, we are aware that we have broken the webbing of life. Somewhere deep within, we, as a human species, do understand the implications of our actions. Each time we break with the connection to all life, we create deeper and deeper patterns of soul loss.

The challenge that arises is two-fold. The first challenge is to stop our self- destructive behavior (and the suffering it will cause for the generations that come after us). To do this, we must collectively wake up from the dream we are in. We must wake up from our denial of the truth.

The second challenge is to creatively, scientifically, spiritually, and with our imaginations find the technology to clean up the disaster we have created. In order to envision the future, we must have the hope and potential for the future to unfold. I believe we have gone to sleep (world soul loss), because we want to freeze out the annihilation/extinction aspect of what we have created as a species. We are in denial of our dark nature. We give our power away to hierarchical, patriarchal systems that obviously no longer have the interests of life continuation in the forefront of decision-making.

In order to effect change, we must first admit we are suffering. Secondly, we are the cause of suffering through egocentricity, ignorance, arrogance, greed, violence and the misuse of power. Next, we must understand the domino effect our actions are having on worldwide soul loss causing distrust, apathy, and the cycling of self-destructive choices. Finally, we must call ourselves home, call ourselves to action through our intention. Through recovery, the four noble truths of Buddhist living state:

> Right intention arises as we understand the systemic nature of life, the interdependence between self and other, mind and body; and right speech arises as we give expression to this with honesty and compassion. Right action, right livelihood, and right effort are no longer abstract notions, but become as immediate and tangible as today's collaboration in clearing the village well (Macy 1991, 137).

In calling ourselves home, we must also look to the nature of our support, to models that exist and are working positively, and to teachers who can assist us in awakening out of the dream. In the introduction to *Coming Back to Life*, His Holiness the Fourteenth Dalai Lama states:

> In our present state of affairs, the very survival of human kind depends on people developing concern for the whole of humanity, not just their own community or nation. The reality of our situation impels us to act and think more clearly. Narrow mindedness and self-centered thinking...will only lead to disaster (Macy and Brown 1998, xvi)

In viewing the epidemic of world soul loss, understand large scale conscious recovery must happen. Seen from the perspective (and the indigenous model) of soul loss and recovery, I suggest the remembering of our ancestral soul is integral to our survival at this point in our history. From the book *Returning to the Teachings*, an exploration of aboriginal justice by Rupert Ross, the author cites a paper written by indigenous elders which explains the view to healing the soul and bringing it back into balance versus using judgment, force, laws and policies to further push, control and regulate behavior.

> People who offend...are to be viewed and related to as people who are out of balance—with themselves, their family, their community and their Creator. A return to balance can best be accomplished through a process of accountability that includes support from the community through teaching and healing. The use of judgment and punishment actually works against the healing process. An already unbalanced person is moved further out of balance (Ross 1996, 171).

In other words, policies and justice-making exist in unity in the indigenous belief that, regardless of the context of things or outward appearances, we all exist in the emotional and spiritual dimensions as well as the mental and physical together. What affects one, affects the entire community. Our connection to one another and indeed to all existence does not exist on one or two levels, i.e., reason and will. Communication, connection and decision-making on the mental level is seen in indigenous cultures as the weakest form. "Real" communication is "felt" not "rational." So heart talking stands as a central ingredient in the healing process" (Ross 1996, 172).

It is through heart talking that the ground is prepared for the soul to come home. In shamanic cultures the heart is the home of creativity, fire, and the imagination. It is the physical, emotional, and spiritual place, in some forms of soul recovery where the remembered soul is blown into the body upon return from the spirit world.

> Shamanism is the medicine of the imagination...The Shamans are the ones who are said to understand, in a spiritual sense, the nexus of the mind, the body, and the soul. Their chief task has always been to heal their people of the ills of humanity (Achterberg 1985, 6).

In the next chapter we will hear the wisdom of post-modern shamans, healers, therapists, and medicine elders. Perhaps they would not name themselves in this way; however, they are our teachers, elders and wisdom keepers. Their words and wisdom differ and provide pathways for soul recovery on a global conscious scale and also provide roadmaps for personal, deep, inner change.

Chapter 3

Heart Talking:
The Wisdom of the Elders

God in the Stew

Is there a human mouth that doesn't
give out soul-sound? Is there love,

a drawing-together of any kind, that
isn't sacred? Every natural dog

sniffs God in the stew. The lion's
paw trembles like a rose petal.

He senses the ultimate spear coming.
In the shepherd's majesty wolves

and lambs tease each other. Look
inside your mind. Do you hear

the crowd gathering? Help coming,
every second. Still you cover

your eyes with mud. Watch the horned
owl. Wash your face. Anyone who

steps into an orchard walks inside
the orchard keeper. Millions

of love-tents bloom on the plain.
A star in your chest says, *None*

of this is outside you. Close your lips
and let the maker of mouths talk,

the one who says *things.*

(By Rumi, Barks 2001, 28)

Curing is remedial and involves fixing whatever outer problem arises, such as patching a tire... Healing is broader, more global and complete. Healing transforms one's life, and often, though not always, produces a physical cure...Healing results from an experience of infinity. While healing, we measure success by increased well-being, by a sense of newfound peace, empowerment, and a feeling of communion with all life (Villoldo 2000, 20).

Elders are our wisdom keepers, our record holders and our heart talkers. Elders are people who speak truths that need to be spoken, not popular truths, sometimes difficult to hear, but yet essential for the health, growth, and balance of the people. Elders hold our recent history in life experiences that they have lived. They are mirrors for us. They are our storytellers, our educators, our healers, our spiritual lineage holders, our mystics and our prophets.

The calling of the elders who speak so eloquently in these next pages came from a vision I had when I was fasting and praying out on the land for four days and nights. I could hear the whispering of their voices as they drew near, but I could not quite make out what they were saying. In a dream it came to me to go ask them to tell me their words so that I could learn and record this wisdom and share it with others.

When spirit conceived this project and planted the seed inside me, I decided to seek elder's council from multi-cultural, multi-spiritual walks of life. I wanted to see if common themes and practices of soul recovery and remembering our true self ran like an underground river across cultures and continents and through different life styles and belief systems. I deliberately declined to make up a questionnaire, feeling that I wanted the interviewees to respond freely to the topic of soul loss and recovery based upon their life experiences and expertise. So I forsook the scientific form and reverted to circular heart talking, an indigenous practice of communication.

The ten elders who answered the call have been incredibly generous with their speech and time to read the transcripts, correct words, and clarify concepts. They have been most encouraging in my writing of this book. [See Appendix A for Heart Talkers' brief biographies.]

There are themes arising in their words that are worthy of note. While each person's voice and spiritual practices are unique, some common insights illuminate the path we are walking together.

It is a commonly held belief by many of these elders that, as a species and as a world, we are in a time of transformation on all levels: in the physical, emotional, mental, and spiritual worlds. Our irresponsible behavior pollutes, kills, destroys, creates "power-over," and recycles patterns of wounding and loss. Each elder speaks about the shadow side of humanity that has, in its denial, numbed us out. In the interviews themes of addictive behaviors, consumerism, materialism, greed, despair, shame and unresolved grief are discussed. Several elders describe the loss of cosmology, and the loss of the sacred in many aspects of our lives. Soul loss is caused through negative behaviors and consequences of splitting, separation and polarization. The refusal of the human species to look at our "dark creature" continues to cause tremendous suffering. Our refusal to grow up and our dependence in recycling the narcissistic wounded nature of our old stories of blame outwardly projected on others is a direct path toward extinction. We are at an intersection in evolution when we can either continue to shrink the soul or grow the soul. If we choose to continue our present behaviors, we will not survive as a species.

We can and do have powerful resources, talents and gifts with which to bridge this river of soul loss. These methods of recovery arise out of the fire of the inspired heart. It is a spiritual bridge that will ford this river, but it must be in balance with the other aspects of the physical, emotional, and mental elements. The healing power of recovery comes through the imagination, through creative visioning, in sacred ceremony, and in community. We can no longer act as isolated personalities. We must lean upon the strength that arises in communal healing and in living a good life for everyone—not just from an individual perspective. Transformation is born out of self-responsible reflection, connection and understanding. Not only do we need to walk this talk now, but we must remember the children and the next generations who will follow us. We must ignite the hearts of our children as we learn how to do this in ourselves. This journey is, firstly, an inner one; then the soul journeys out to the world to manifest change. We are the healers and the midwives. We are the change-makers we have been waiting for.

In the interviews that follow, I have included material from elders whose beliefs and spiritual practices differ from my own. I conducted these interviews deliberately and with an open heart so that, through dialogue, contrasting spiritual practices and therapies could be heard. I believe in open communication and tolerance of all approaches to healing ways. If I had only included interviews with elders who practice spirituality parallel to the tradition I was taught, it would have been akin to "cooking the book." I am more interested in exploring the ways in which healing, change, and lasting relationships can happen. I believe it is in this way that we can truly hear one another. When we hear one another from our hearts, differences dissolve, and we find ourselves on the same journey.

List of Heart Talkers

1. Kay Cordell Whitaker   October 3, 2000
   Santa Fe, New Mexico

2. Don Alberto Tazto, and Silvia Reynoso   March 14, 2001
   Rumipampa, Ecuador, South America

3. Luisah Teish   June 14, 2001
   Oakland, California

4. Patricia Whitebuffalo   June 15, 2001
   Soquel, California

5. Anita Barrows   June 17, 2001
   Berkeley, California

6. Matthew Fox   June 20, 2001
   Oakland, California

7. Sandra Ingerman   September 19, 2001
   Santa Fe, New Mexico

8. Arielle Guttman   September 20, 2001
   Santa Fe, New Mexico

9. Sam Beeler   July 31, 2004
   Paterson, New Jersey

10. Judith Schmidt   November 23, 2001
    Goldens Bridge, New York

INTERVIEW WITH
KAY CORDELL WHITAKER

October 3, 2000

Santa Fe, New Mexico

JE: *In your work and training, how do you experience soul loss?*

KW: It is epidemic. I rarely meet anyone in this culture who does not suffer from it. From the point of view of the indigenous people who taught me (Chea and Domano Hetaka; their culture is in eastern Peru where it borders Brazil--a mixture of the Amazon and the highland post-Inca cultures), we have a totality of our being, our spirit, that they refer to as our "song." It is not something that is a sound necessarily, it is a poetic reference to describe the vastness and the ancientness, the complexity and the beauty of who and what we are as an entity, as human beings. In our totality we have experienced the universe for eons and eons and eons; who knows in how many different places and ways? We have taken form and joined in countless societies, cultures, species and here we are now within the human species. From the Hetaka's point of view this era, this time on our planet, is a critical one, a critical piece of history. It is not quite like any other point in the history of this planet or within our species.

JE: *Why is that?*

KW: Many things in our universe move in cycles. We repeat cycles. We have had different cycles or eras that we have lived in. The Hopi refer to them as "worlds." The Hetakas talk about them as eras: cycles in which humans lived in a particular place, maybe a continent that is not up now, and a group of people who were together in that time and place focusing on certain aspects of existence. The era that we are in right now is coming to an end. In the ending of any of these eras, there is a massive change: there is the breaking down of what has been, the building up of something new, and there is always a crossover time. We are in the crossover time now. Because of how we have chosen to live in this last era and what we have chosen to concentrate on, we have created for ourselves a momentum of extremes, more so than in previous times. There have been other eras where humanity as a group has used its trust (that had been given to it by Creator and by the spirit world) and used its knowledge and its opportunities to bring imbalance to the places they lived in—thus, inadvertently harming the planet and destroying each other (e.g., Atlantis and Lemuria ended up in the breaking down of cultures that had became highly dysfunctional). But according to my grandparents, the Hetakas and their tribe, we in our modern culture have perfected this going out of balance. We have carried the experiment out to its farthest end. We have lived out the possibilities and potentials into the most "negative" ways that we could dream up, all of them all at once as much as we could do, we have done it to perfection. And in doing so, in this cycle of time, this era is coming to its end. We have created radical polarization. In this polarization, we not only see the world as having these poles of extreme negativity (e.g., evil, bad, wrong, less-than), but also their opposites: extreme rightness, goodness, correctness, God-ness, holiness, better-than. By polarizing everything to such an exaggeration and living out those possibilities, those potentials, we have fractured ourselves.

The Hetakas describe our era, this experiment, as a "backwards turning wheel." They say there are two basic energies in our universe. Because we want matter and measurement, we have a place that has three dimensions. That means we have to have polarization— we have to have an up and a down. We end up with pairs such as male and female. Although there is duality in polarization, we have pulled it apart into such extremes that we have literally been trying to manifest our belief in separation; and this action is ripping the world apart. In duality we have an energy that turns clockwise, and we have an energy that turns counter-clockwise. Yin and Yang— one energy builds things and creates; the other energy takes things apart, destroys. Neither is good or bad or right or wrong. They are simply the motor of our universe.

From the Hetakas' point of view, our modern western culture can be easily traced back six or seven thousand years. It has had its little nuances here and there, but it is the same culture.

JE: *Would this be one era—this seven thousand year cycle?*

KW: Reaching back to 10,000 B.C. as they see it, an era is about 12,000 years. Those numbers, in turn, relate to other group cycles— there is a 26,000 year cycle, and we are on one-half of that; and now we are coming to see the other half of the 26,000 year cycle. As a culture that is designed and based on one energy, the energy that turns backward, the one that takes apart, means everything it is and does as it moves through time tears things apart, tears itself apart as that wheel turns. It is tearing everything in its path apart. We as a race have gone into the exploration of the phenomenon of this energy to every possible depth. These backwards turning energies by themselves are destructive. Living them becomes an exploration of force and power that becomes "power over." And this is what we have been living.

JE: *On the physical, the emotional and the spiritual levels?*

KW: On all levels—this is what our culture is all about, what it is based on. The era is coming to its end. It's on its very last turn. The wheel has fallen apart through the years; we pick up the pieces; we try to put Humpty Dumpty back together, it turns a little bit more. It is now at a place where it is falling apart so completely that it cannot be put back together again. It has done its thing; it's over. And as much as we try to pick up the old pieces and make the old world again, it is not going to happen. It can't be put back. What we must do, as we are crossing from one era into the next, is to build something brand new, to create brand new pieces, new concepts with the opposite energy—the positive clockwise turning energy that creates things and holds them into creation. A true balance of all life needs to have both energies. But as we move from one extreme and are in the crossover, we need to create pieces of positive turning energy, use the wheel to begin the creation of the next era, and find a way to develop culture out of new concepts. In a positive turning wheel energy, the underlying dynamic is win-win. Everybody is equal. There is no power over, no self-importance.

JE: *Would you say that duality comes closer together then?*

KW: Yes, but only from a certain perspective—it's like the ebbing of the tides. There has to be a mending of the web. What we have done to the web is literally rip it apart. In order to exist, the web has to be intact. You can't reconstruct it the way it has been. It is a very dysfunctional web, but it has to be developed; and we have to figure out what the pieces are to develop and mend the web.

The web of the entire culture has been torn. Little children brought into the world are taught the ways of the world. Our culture has been teaching them the broken, torn web—and we tear their web, we injure them, we tear them apart. In doing this, we rip them in ways that become very difficult to mend. Quite literally, pieces of their being are removed from their spirit.

From the Hetakas' point of view, soul loss means that we have taken a hunk, a piece of our spirit being, a part that has gotten injured or traumatized (a part that doesn't want to play this game anymore) and ripped it out of ourselves and sent it someplace where it is safe. We send it out into the spirit realms where the spirits can take care of it, and it doesn't have to continue suffering the injuries that traumatized it.

JE: *In their terminology, Kay, when that happens, does that soul part or fragment that is going into the realm of the spirits become frozen at a certain age (for example, if the trauma happened at age three or five or anywhere along the continuum)?*

KW: Yes, it does not have a continued "growth" of its own. It stops its identification with its totality, growth, or interaction with the world and becomes frozen. It goes off to a place where it can be protected; and, it often doesn't even know where it is.

JE: *And does that soul fragment carry the trauma with it?*

KW: Yes.

JE: *So it remembers the trauma even though it is frozen in space?*

KW: They aren't completely frozen as if dead, but many times they just isolate themselves as if in suspended animation. There is no awareness, no growth; it's like they go to sleep. They just numb out; they are in a place where they know they are safe and where there are spirits that will take care of them. They remain there until the person that they belong to dies and they can reunite again. Or somewhere in that person's life they find a way to contact this piece and find a way to accept the piece back into their own being, into their life. For the person that has torn out this piece, they literally have a hole; if you see their auric field, there is a hole there; and we do all kinds of things to try to make up the difference.

We develop all kinds of psychological systems, programs which my grandparents called "masks." These masks are a way of interacting with the world. We develop all kinds of masks to try to cover up the hole, to take care of the business that that piece of spirit would have been taking care of if it were still there. Where there is a hole, there is an underlying constant ache, an emptiness, a loss, and there is nothing you can do in a human life to make that emptiness or pain go away. As long as the piece is gone and the hole is there, the ache is there. We do all kinds of things in our culture to try to numb it or to try to fill the hole, such as addictions. We are a very addictive society, and we'll go through any number of addictions trying to fill that hole. We go through relationship addictions, we go through alcohol, drugs, cigarettes, food, work, thinking addictions, televisions, sex, everything, you name it. We will just try one after the other to see what's going to fill the hole up and make things right again. And it doesn't; none of it works; the hole is always there.

People in our culture have many of these holes. We've had so much trauma, so much stress, so many abusive situations that we've put ourselves into or someone else has thrust us into, we don't know how to cope with the parts of us that just say, "that's it; this is the last time I am every doing this; I'm leaving right now." And we tear the piece out and off it goes. When we look at so many people in our culture psychically, in a medicine way, and see their aura, it's just one hole and bruise after the other.

JE: *Do you see those as dark spots—the holes?*

KW: Sometimes they look like a dark spot. In my grandparents' teachings, when we look at somebody in a medicine way, we're receiving information about what is going on with them; and the information is translated inside us using our own inner symbology. So we'll get a picture or a sense or a feeling of what's there and it will come to us in our own symbols. So for me personally, sometimes I see a dark spot, sometimes I literally see a big hole, an indentation. Sometimes it looks like it's been sealed over with cement, kind of plastered up; other times, it looks open and raw, oozy, dripping energy and life. It's so open that it has created a big tear in the outer edge of the aura so that the people become very susceptible to any sort of unfortunate energy and negative quality energy floating around in the same area. It gravitates straight to that open sore and works its way right into their being.

JE: *Would you call that possession?*

KW: No. I'm not sure anybody has a real definition or understanding of what possession is, or even if it actually exists. Our environments are extremely crowded and polluted with the energies we have sent out from ourselves. What could be floating around could be the energy of a headache, a stomach flu, a thought-form full of fear, or anger, or detrimental electromagnetic energies. It could be any number of different things. When it seeks its way into somebody through a hole, they don't notice that it is actually alien to them. They can't tell that it belonged to somebody else, and that they don't have to accept it. Once it touches them and gets into their body, they think it's theirs; so they accept it; it comes right on in and mixes with the whole system. They make it part of their agenda of the moment; they think it's theirs. So, if it was the stomach flu, all of a sudden, they've got it. If it's a thought-form full of anger, then it pushes all their own buttons for their own agendas or masks programs that they are carrying around that have to do with anger. That button gets pushed and they are up and running doing their own little anger number having no concept that it is somebody else's thought, somebody else's trip—and they caught it.

JE: *And, in turn, it activated that part of themselves that's being covered over. So behind the button that gets pushed are the actual wounds. Behind the mask is there the loss?*

KW: The loss is always there. Because the holes are there and because they are gaping wounds, they are losing energy. The person's own life sustenance is dribbling out, oozing out, gushing out—it depends on the person and the wound. And because it's open, they are very susceptible and vulnerable to anything that's floating around. It could be something that was purposefully aimed, it could be something left behind by somebody who isn't even there anymore. It can be anything, and they will take it on thinking it is their own; and they'll act it out.

The pieces we throw away can be very interesting. The whole phenomenon of soul loss--how it happens, what pieces get thrown away and why--can be very prophetic. Consider, for example, the case of a very talented child with a lot of gifts, very intelligent, who is growing up in an abusive family where fighting takes place, where the parents really put down the child saying he/she is no good, stupid and inferior; and every creative act is trash--it doesn't take too many of those events before a piece of the spirit says, "I just can't do it anymore." For that child the piece is the most creative piece. It's the part that wanted to express itself in its wholeness and was not allowed. It was tortured when expressing itself. So that is the piece of the spirit that gets ripped out and sent off. Meanwhile, the person has a sense of knowing, a holographic knowingness, that they are creative. The ability and the knowledge is an echo in their body. The part of them that had the tools isn't there right now. So no matter what they do in their lives to try to access it, no matter how badly and deeply they have a drive to be creative and do something in that realm, they can't.

JE: *Tell me, Kay, when the soul part makes that choice to fragment and to go away, is it the wisdom of the oversoul that is taking the action? How does the fragmentation actually take place according to your understanding?*

KW: From the Hetakas' traditions, they call our "song" the totality of who and what we are, our entity. It's immense, extremely vast and extremely ancient. It's been a number of places, has all this knowledge and these gifts, has lots and lots and lots of memory. It's also connected to everything in the universe, and it can access those connections to retrieve more information and more experience whenever it needs to. This huge entity that we are, this totality, when we come into a physical body to live a life, we purposely forget just how big it is, how old, where it's been and all its memories. In order to focus on something that's in this life, something we want to achieve here, we have to temporarily forget about how big we are, where we've been, and all those pieces of information. We are holographic: what traumatizes the part affects the whole. When the part can't cope, the totality makes the decision. To ask anybody—a child, an adult if they consciously have any awareness of how or when they tore these pieces out, very few people can pinpoint it at all—it's not conscious here and now in the 3-D physical world. It's an activity that takes place on a greater level of where we interface with a far vaster perspective.

JE: *So, when that decision is made, what happens to the remainder of the song when part of the song is gone?*

KW: There's that sense of loss; there's a sense of always mourning and not knowing what you are mourning for. There's an emptiness and you are not quite sure how it got into you; what exactly is empty; why; what's that about? There is a sense of "should be able to" yet there is something there the person can't do, can't accomplish, they are disabled, they become dysfunctional; their web is torn. There is a big empty spot. Something's been ripped out. We do our best to function without the missing pieces. That is such an individual thing—some people manage pretty well and other people are very crippled—the loss is too big, is too great, the piece they threw away was way too vital.

JE: *And then would you go into clinical diagnosis such as schizophrenia, psychosis or neurosis?*

KW: That kind of diagnosis can happen when there is a huge fracture, and the kind of pieces that got thrown away were the parts of one's being that one needs in order to have mental function, to think a thought all the way through, to be able to correlate data, to be able to tell what our reality is all about, or what dimensions of reality we are in. When our web gets that fractured, we lose the pieces that do that kind of defining. We can't function within the world any more. We are no longer able to hang onto a functional definition for ourselves or what reality is and our place in it. We have lost it. We have these phrases about having "lost our marbles," "a taco short of a full plate," "not playing with a full deck," "trippin'," "a mind blower," and that kind of thing.

JE: *There is a lot of that kind of dialogue in our culture.*

KW: And it's not that far off. Someone who has that much damage easily would be diagnosed as borderline schizophrenic or paranoid schizophrenic.

JE: *So, I'm just going to diverge for a second here, because I think there is an interesting question about people who go into these different dimensions. In spiritual work, we often cross over into other dimensions. What is the difference between a mystic, a prophet or a healer versus a paranoid schizophrenic?*

KW: Very often someone who is a paranoid schizophrenic or somebody who is borderline, has lost pieces of the linear mind that holds this 3-D reality box in place. We have to have a certain amount of the linear structure in how we perceive the world around us and how we perceive ourselves. The other part of our being-ness is the non-linear—we have the linear and the non-linear. We have to have both; both exist in this universe and both exist in us—we need them both. We need to learn how to use both together. Someone who has become schizophrenic has lost the use of the linear part of their Being. What is left of their linear mind can't hold itself together. The person no longer sees any borderline between what is linear and what is non-linear. They cannot distinguish the difference. In the non-linear is where we interact with other worlds, other realities, other dimensions, the spirit worlds (i.e., everything we define as outside of time-space, moving into the spiritual realms, interacting with non-physical intelligences).

We are also part of a linear-ness, a 3-D linear-ness. Without the constraints of that 3-D linear box inside ourselves and outside, we wouldn't be able to tell what's what. All the different worlds start melting into each other, and the point of awareness bounces from one world experience to another haphazardly. We have all these definitions for the box- like coordinates. Without the linear part of the mind, we don't have any framework or anchor; there is no reference point. The focus point of the attention drifts and bounces, and we end up in a world over there for a few moments, then bounce back here in this world, then bounce back into the past or this dimension or this spirit world or even talk with an entity from that world.

In the case of a mystic, healer, prophet or shaman, their linear minds are disciplined. They understand the dynamics of the non-linear mind, and they know how to use their linear and non-linear minds together. They have full control over the directing of their attention and can aim it anywhere they want within the linear and the non-linear without distraction for as long as they wish. They are anchored, stable and are totally aware of all the reference points.

JE: *Would you say that the emotional body or the auric field is a bridge in this case between the matrix of the linear box of the mind and the other dimensions, the non-linear? Where does the emotional body come into play in bridging?*

KW: Our song includes our whole auric field, our physical body, and all of the different things we label as our subtle or spirit bodies. These different "bodies" are not in any way separate or separable—we cannot pull them apart from each other. What other belief systems might define as an emotional body or a mental body are a range of frequencies. Our whole auric self is within this egg-sphere shape—the edge of which sits outside the physical body, its interior penetrates through and is part of our physical body. One range of frequencies of this totality is our physical body, and the next range of frequencies would be what we define as the emotional body. The next range would be the mental body; the next would be one of the spiritual body levels. There are many many different ranges of these frequencies, and we are designed to operate interactively within all of them all the time.

In our modern western culture, we have learned how to utilize the emotional frequencies and the more linear aspects of the mental frequencies—that's where we concentrate our activity. We have our physical functioning; it's on automatic. We don't have to worry about generating it—it's just there and most folks don't pay any attention to what it is doing. Most of us have very little sensation or awareness of how healthy or unhealthy we are or what our thought patterns are manifesting in any given part of the physical body. We are just not paying attention at all. What we are focusing on are the frequencies of the emotional and mental levels—that is where the concentration of activity is. The Hetakas taught me how to tune into the different levels so when you look at the emotional frequency range, you are going to see the emotional body and the activity taking place. Now most people in this culture have learned how to concentrate their activity in the front of their physical body from about their chest to their forehead. It goes out about a foot from the body, and all the activity they have is primarily confined right there.

In the mental levels, it's in that same location. And the two interact with each other. If you watch the two levels, people might start with a mental/verbal thought, and you see that activity. If you look immediately to the emotional level, you'll see some kind of counterpart activity happening emotionally. Very often it happens the other way around—you'll have an emotional uprising and it will stir mental thoughts. You'll see that same copy cat activity between the two levels.

But if you go to the next grouping of higher frequencies, which are the more spiritual levels, there is nothing taking place. Sometimes you'll see a very very thin light color wisp taking up some of the auric space; it never moves; it never changes. There is no activity happening there. Most of the people in our culture are not trained on those levels. They have no idea of what to do with them or how to use them. And so they just sit as if vacant. There are a few professions where a gifted or trained person can develop the spiritual level of activity and learn how to use it interactively with the other levels.

JE: *Wouldn't that be not inhabiting your song fully (from the Hetakas' perspective)?*

KW: That is a very interesting way to put it.

JE: *There are empty levels where nothing is happening?*

KW: They are empty of activity. They have pulled all their attention out of them and they are pretending the auric spaces don't exist. It is kind of shocking when you see it. When you look at very tiny children before they have been programmed socially (e.g., one, two, three years old), they are using all these different levels. The edge of their own auric space is way out here—two, three, four feet out—a beautiful round shape defining the edge of their aura, without any holes. There are no darts or things sticking to it. It's not leaking and on all levels they are using the whole space. They don't concentrate it only in front of their chest and face; it's all the way down around their feet and back and there's all this color and this big activity is going every which way. All the levels interact with each other as the children are running and playing. They are all excited, and they are streaming this excitement out into the world. They leave a trail behind them, these waves and with gushes of colors bursting out. It's just so free and spontaneous, so full of passion--so alive!

And then you see kids a little bit older who have been culturalized. They have taken on all the rules, all the boxes, all the should's and they are not using the spiritual levels any more. Their aura is sucked into a foot from their body, and it is very strictly defined, often flat surfaces. It's as if they are trying to make it into a box. You don't see the fullness of activity any more. They are not using their aura all the way down to their feet; they are starting to cut themselves off from the Mother Earth.

JE: *Once we become aware that there is loss, how can we consciously call that part of ourselves home or work with that part of ourselves?*

KW: Most people in our culture do not have the emotional stamina to do it by themselves; that is, the stamina to mentally and emotionally will the parts back and be able to be whole again. We certainly do not have any cultural thought-form that covers this realm. We are not trained; there is nothing in our schooling that covers this kind of concept. Most people in our culture don't have any idea whatsoever that spirit loss exists.

From the Hetakas' tradition, what they usually do as a remedy is to go on a spirit journey. The person with soul loss (if they are physically capable) goes on a spirit journey for themselves. There are other traditions where other people go for you; they do the journey and bring back pieces for you and try to help you reunite. In the Hetakas' tradition, they only do that if someone is unconscious or totally incapacitated.

So, assuming that the person is capable and conscious, the remedy would be to go on a spirit journey to the land of the animal spirits, using your own spirit helpers, and your power animal in particular, as a guide to take you to the lost pieces. Because you intend to do this, this sends a message, a rippling out, into the spirit worlds and wherever these lost parts have been kept, whatever world, whatever realm, in whose-ever protection—they are all brought down to the land of the animal spirits for the meeting. So when we go there with our own helpers and our power animals as a guide, we are going to run into them—the meeting has been arranged and they are all there. In the journey, we take the majority of the spiritual essence of our song out of our physical body. With our attention and our intention, we aim ourselves to the land of the animal spirits. This is a spiritual realm where the spirits of animals tend to collect between lives. When they are in their own spirit form, when they need to congregate in that way, this is the spirit realm that is most dominant in that activity. So that's where we head in the journey.

There are traditions in how to get there, how to find that world. So we go through that process, go to that land of the animal spirits with our helpers guiding us down whatever path we need to take to find the pieces. In the Hetakas' tradition, it's not important what the pieces look like. We can encounter anything in the spirit realm. What we perceive is our own inner symbology trying to define the experience. It could look like anything. When we encounter a lost spirit piece, we may see it as a piece of ourself at different ages. We may see it as something we remember from a certain age such as a doll, a toy, something that was important to us. It may take an abstract form that doesn't mean anything to us at all at first. That's all OK. It doesn't matter what it looks like or if you actually remember anything about what this image is and what the symbologies are. What's important is the "feeling-tone-recognition," which is a quality of knowing that whatever you have encountered has the essence of you, has your soul's signature. It has the signature of a missing piece of you.

JE: *So, again, it's back to frequency.*

KW: Yes, there's a frequency. Every individual, every soul has its own frequency signature; that's what defines it. It's unique; it's absolutely unique in the universe. So when you run across your lost piece, it's going to have your signature and you're going to feel it. We take this piece, whatever its appearance happens to be, we accept it without any judgments. We try to put the history aside. Usually a piece is torn out because there has been trauma, injury, abuse; something awful has happened. With the Hetakas, they don't have any concept of judgment and condemnation. They observe and discern, but they don't judge. They don't even have a word in their language for judgment.

JE: *Then the lens is discernment?*

KW: Yes, the key is in discernment instead of judgment. You look clearly at the details, you analyze and discern, and you make a decision from that. Judgment and condemnation do not exist for the Hetakas. As they taught me, when we go down into this world to do this process, we have to set the judgment aside. We go in with the whole intention of taking all judgment and setting it aside; it doesn't belong in that spirit world. So judging yourself, condemning yourself, for throwing a piece of yourself away years ago—you just can't do it. It doesn't make any sense. You can't judge the piece for leaving; you just set that aside. You can't judge the people involved in the initial event that may have been abusive. Certainly they shouldn't have done those things, but by putting the judgment aside, it doesn't mean you are condoning those hurtful actions, you are just not condemning the people. When we condemn and we judge, we are throwing darts and injuring; we are throwing condemnation at someone else or something else.

JE: *And would you say we stay connected when we attach with judgment?*

KW: Absolutely. Every time you throw a dart, there is a cord. You are tied just like the whaling ship's harpoon to the whale; you are tied, and you are there for a nice long ride.

Judging produces a cord of unbalanced energies that binds you to what you have judged. In approaching a soul piece that you lost, you accept it just as it is. Who and what it is and all its history—it just is. All the condemning is put aside. And you bring the piece into your chest, into your Being and let it melt. Let it melt back into your Being. Bring it to your chest, your heart area, because that is the most important thing to connect. The lost piece has to reestablish its connection to your center which is in your heart. So, bring it to the heart and let it melt back in, accepting and loving, reuniting and feeling. Feel what it's like to have the piece back, to connect up again. Here is something that you have been out of touch with for years. There is a familiarity and there is an unfamiliarness. The longer you've been without that piece, the more you have learned to live without it. And so getting it back can feel awkward sometimes.

JE: *And what happens to the mask at that time? Does it dissolve or shift with the vibrational reuniting?*

KW: We create a hole in tossing a piece off. We create at least one mask to cover the hole, to try to take care of the jobs that that piece used to do. Just because we have the spirit piece back, the masks are not going to quietly walk off and go away. Masks, our programs, are just not like that. We have been living with the masks a long time and we are very addicted to them, to the patterns. So when we get the piece back, the masks usually don't like the idea. They were created to fill the hole and pretend to make up the differences. The soul piece isn't supposed to be there from their point of view. They are going to try to send the piece off again. So whatever it is that is their job, their agenda, their belief system, these masks are going to use that to get up into your face, into your ears, get your attention, get in the driver's seat. They're going to run their little tapes; they're going to babble whatever it takes to get you to listen to put the piece back. "Send it back; send it back, send it back. It doesn't belong here; it shouldn't be here." Whatever you are going to listen to and believe, that is what the masks are going to say because they're going to try and get their own way. They think they're right. They were created to help you survive, to take care of a drastic situation. The masks see the world in their own peculiar distorted way. One of the main points of view of the masks is that there is a hole there and that the masks' job is to take care of the hole and its tasks. You are not supposed to have the missing piece back. The masks see it all as life threatening.

Jane Ely, Ph.D., D.Min.

JE: *How does the soul part begin to integrate on a conscious level in the energy field and in our psyche?*

KW: It does on all the levels. The soul piece in a holographic way has all the levels, the seeker usually feels a difference when they come back—often a sense of being fuller, of having achieved a reestablishment or gaining back of something of themselves that they haven't had for a long time. There is a sense of remembering something larger, of great value in themselves, of ownership again. Sometimes, they say they now feel settled, that they have a sense of peace that was not there before.

We often retrieve a number of pieces on one journey. It takes awhile for the reuniting to complete, for all the readjustments to anchor. The longer one has been without a piece the more readjustment there is that needs to happen. Very often, people from our modern culture get some pieces back and, within a week, have tossed one or more of them off again. It's our habit; it's what we are used to. The person then needs to go back on another spirit journey, go back to the land of the animal spirits, and retrieve the piece again. Sometimes, it takes two-three-four journeys retrieving the same piece, bringing it back, going through the same process and by then we reestablish a sustainable integration. It just needs to be repeated until the soul pieces stabilize. Every one of the parts, pieces, levels and aspects of our Being adjusts and accepts to facilitate the reunion. Very few people I have worked with have been able to go on just one journey to bring pieces back and have them all stay.

JE: *Once there is stabilization, what do you notice shifts in the person?*

KW: Even if the piece is only with them a short time, while it is back with them, there's an energy increase. The quality of their energy lightens, there's a sense of wholeness and balance and a sense of stability that was not there before. It's as if they used to have a house that had two pillars trying to hold up four corners and now they have four pillars. Their house used to be on sand; now it's on rock. They have a quality of smoothness, a decrease in agitation replaced by strength and fortitude that had been absent. They grasp a bigger perspective. There's an increased willingness to pursue life and push through their old boundaries. Their abilities to perform normal daily life activities increase tremendously. For example, a person might have had an enormous amount of creativity that was thrown away when they were little. As an adult, they are unable to do work that involves creativity. They are unable to perform; they don't have all the tools. They get themselves hired and they can only do half a job. They have a whole life of repeated struggle as long as the pieces are not there.

JE: *Let's look at the larger picture the Hetakas were talking about in terms of the wheel's going in the opposite direction ending this era. Do you see that the epidemic proportions of soul loss are part of this dissolution that we are going through? Do you see it as a natural way that we have to dissolve in order for this era to end?*

KW: Breaking apart is a phenomenon of the culture that's based on a backwards turning wheel. The culture itself is based on separation: it's about tearing things apart, about being in pieces, about torn webs, things dysfunctional, power over, co-dependent relationships. As the wheel falls apart things get extreme. Whatever we have developed as a creation, whatever kinds of processes, functions, types and ways of being that we have—everything becomes accentuated the closer we get to the end. As that wheel is disintegrating, it's doing it in a big way! Things go out in a bang! I think we're noticing it more. Now that we have a lot of interaction with other cultures and their way of looking at the world and their kinds of medicine, we have a way of describing what has been happening to our people. We have been doing this—tearing pieces out of ourselves and sending them off—for thousands of years. And we've been doing it in an ever increasing pace. Right now, it's probably at the peak of its epidemic, and that's because of the intensity of the culture as it's spinning its last rounds of the wheel.

This accelerated calamity is a natural consequence, a natural way, for the culture to dissolve. But the era ending is not dependent on whether or not the culture has ended. It will end when it's time all on its own.

Our Songs as humans have no dissolving to do. Our masks, now, are a different story—we need to wake up and break free of them in order to build and be part of the next era that is coming. As long as the masks are there, the breaking apart of the culture accentuates and stimulates them. Ultimately, with enough destruction and death and time, "nature" will provide a way for us to "break away" from all the masks. It's up to us whether we do it ourselves right now with less destruction or wait and let the dance be directed by "nature."

JE: *Did the Hetakas believe that the year 2012 or 2013 was the end of this time period?*

KW: They don't have an exact date like the Mayans do on their calendar but it's about the same time. Their way of detecting the time is more in terms of moments in a similar way to the Hopi prophecies that have a whole list of things that describe the end times are coming. And then if we don't start cleaning up our act and getting a little spiritual, learning more about humanity, kindness, love, connectedness to Earth and all those sorts of things—then these warnings happen. Then if we still don't clean up our act, the next thing is going to happen. It is shown as one step after the other.

JE: *And did they actually talk about those steps?*

KW: A good number of them. Yes. Most of them have come about. [*Really, such as?*] Well, they talk about the white man coming—that's a major marker. "Wasicu"—it means "one who eats the fat" from when the Lakota first encountered white people. The Lakota people were being gracious, and they invited the white man to their teepee for dinner. They had baskets and pots with different food. Fat was a very vital part of their diet—they were eating deer, buffalo, elk, and you don't get huge hunks of fat on those animals. So the fat pieces were really prized, and they were always shared. The fat pieces were in this one dish all piled up (sort of like a candy dish). And, as they were eating and passing the food trays around, all the Lakota know that they get one little piece and there will be enough for everybody there to get some. But when they put it in front of the white people, the white people ate the whole dish "Wasicu"—it was the foretelling of who and what the white people were all about and what they were going to do. [*They take what they want.*] That's right—they'll eat everything.

JE: *What other signs were the beginning of the end of the turning backwards wheel?*

KW: The disappearing of the wild life in the forests, the changes in weather. They are very descriptive and come in a specific order. The rains changing is a sign. Any of us going to their neighborhood would never notice that there's less rain. For them, they notice it in a very big way. The water levels of all the rivers, even in the rainy season, are not what they used to be; the snow in the mountains is much less, there are some mountain peaks that used to always be covered with snow, and in the summer they lose their snow now. That's another one of the signs.

Specific species dying out, comets of a particular description, celestial groupings, airplanes—the invention of things that go in the sky with increased levels of pollution, the declining quality of water and aquatic species dying off. They can tell the pollution level of the air. When certain frogs disappeared, they knew that it was time for their elders to leave the village and go out into the world and pass out the knowledge to the rest of the world. Their knowledge is what they kept very secure, very secret. They were almost a xenophobic tribe; they really kept away from almost everybody. Some of their local neighbors are very peaceful, matriarchal like they are. There has been interaction and intermarriage, and there has been a sharing of things with the people high up the mountains in the post-Inca groups.

But the other tribes who moved in, the new neighbors they call them, like the Jívaro, they are very aggressive, violent, and they just stay away from them. They have always moved back and given their territory away. They won't go to war over that. Groups like the Jívaros would go out and kill their neighbors so they would have a spiritual sacrifice; there was a lot of human sacrifice going on. The Jívaros are the head hunters, the head shrinkers. They knew there was no interaction there. Interacting with people who have views that are very different would alter what they had and their belief was they had to keep their knowledge intact, perfectly intact, because some day it would be needed by the rest of the world. So they retreated and retreated and when the white man came, they were very happy to go as far up into the hills and cliffs as they needed to and let the Jívaros stay on the river to greet the white people. There are all kinds of horror stories about when the white people were first coming up the rivers and they encountered the Jívaros and other people of the same cultural group, the headhunters.

JE: *In their way of thinking and their perspective, do they believe that there is the way of healing and recovering and staying in balance as this wheel is flying apart?*

KW: Absolutely. For them, the most important thing that one can learn is to know who you are, to know who and what your song is. This knowing of the feeling quality enables you to turn your attention into the unique frequency of your being and own it, be it, identify with it, live from there and observe the world from there. The mask patterns can't exist in that frequency range of the truth of living from one's own song. The mask and the song have very different qualities and frequencies. They just don't exist simultaneously in our conscious awareness. You are either in your song or you are buried in your masks. This means that either you are awake in the now moment or your masks are controlling you. The more attention you spend being in your song and coming from your song (in that place of clarity), the weaker the masks become. They get further and further away, and the cords to them begin to disintegrate and eventually they are just gone. That's what real freedom is. And it's what we need as individuals, as a society and as a species in order to survive.

When you are in the driver's seat of your song, you have control of your attention and your decisions. Your life energy increases and is under your direction. When your masks are in the driver's seat, you are running on automatic pilot and subject to any whim of your mask's agenda. You've given away all your power to your masks.

The Hetakas are very non-warring people. Their traditions, their medicine techniques are what they call "non-warring." It's win-win. There is no blame and no attacking your masks. You don't blame yourself because you have masks. Humans as a species are inclined to develop masks in their different cultures. We have done it in our modern culture to perfection. We are absolute masters of the art of mask-making and wearing. So for us it is a rougher ride requiring more effort, more dedication to unplugging the masks. But the bottom line is to always go back to the feeling quality of your song. Who are you? What is the feeling? What does it mean to be you? What are the qualities that exist inside that song? What's the song's history? What's that magnificence? And identify with it, live it, be it and own it.

When we can do that, then whatever is happening, no matter how chaotic society is, no matter how horrific the falling apart, we have a place of stability, centeredness and clarity. From the state of stability, we can observe the world and interact with it. When we have that perspective what we observe is much fuller and clearer and undistorted. When we are living in the masks and buried in those automatic patterns, those patterns are what is in the driver's seat and give us a very distorted picture. We don't see what reality is; we see what the masks want us to see. So when we get those masks pried off our face and they are not running the show, then we are awake, coming from our song, from truth.

JE: *Is there any other comment or direction that comes to mind before we close?*

KW: From the Hetakas' point of view, to know one's song in its richest capacity and to be able to fully explore it in all of its avenues, its vastness and ancientness, you have to have your soul pieces back. You have to have all the pieces back and they have to be accepted absolutely unconditionally. You have to accept yourself unconditionally. When all those parts and pieces are back, you've thrown away all the judgments of all the issues surrounding them, and you feel and explore yourself in that totality—then you have the opportunity to really know yourself, to know the fullness of self. Without the parts and pieces you will never know the fullness of the truth you carry.

This is very vital work. It is one of the first core processes. Even in their own puberty rites, soul retrieval is part of the process. They go on their power animal journey to learn who the power animal is and develop an active, conscious relationship with that being. They learn more about their own song and how to explore it. They clear out and open up their energy system. And they go on a soul retrieval to find whatever pieces they may have lost in their young life, to bring that back and reintegrate it. They learn the process to be able to use it through their whole life, so that if they do have trauma, they know how to cure it for themselves. They can always go back and hunt for the lost pieces.

Sometimes we "lose" pieces of ourselves that aren't exactly soul pieces; it isn't an actual piece of our own entity that we have ripped out. It's something a little more subtle. For instance, our "power," our "personal power," our own inner authority to be able to be who we are and make our own decisions and trust in ourselves. When we've had the kind of life we typically live in this modern western culture with all of its abuses and attacks and its demeaning pounding quality on us, we may give away our power to other people—to systems, to beliefs, to our masks, to whoever and whatever is out there we give away our power.

JE: *Is that not termed "soul loss"?*

KW: Not by the Hetakas. That is a little different. Soul loss for them is when you literally rip out a piece of your entity/being and send it off. When we give away our power without having torn out a piece with it (you can do both at the same time, but we often give away power without tearing out a piece), we create energy cords to whoever/whatever we gave the power to. [*What if it's a belief system?*] We create a cord to the thought form of that belief system, and we are sending our life energy and our attention, giving it away, continually. It's a hose that is always on and until we learn how to cut it, it's there. So when we're giving this power away, here are

80

these cords, these hoses that are siphoning off our life energy. We are voluntarily making these cords, giving away this energy. We are "leaky." In a lot of ways it's similar to sending away a piece of our spirit because we are refusing to acknowledge that these are our cords. We refuse to take responsibility for it. We're afraid of it.

JE: *So when we are doing that and we recognize that we have attached to, say, a belief system, let's say in this case, a certain lifestyle (where mom and dad are working full time and the kids are latchkey kids and the important thing is the BMW and computer in every room)—would you say that those are cords attached to a belief system of consumerism or materialism?*

KW: Oh yes.

JE: *And we are leaking our energy which may or may not be a case for soul loss?*

KW: It's not specifically what the Hetakas would identify as a soul loss, but it is definitely giving away your power. You're blinding and dogmatically believing in a certain thing, a certain system, a way of being and doing that requires you to feed your attention and energy to that system in an inappropriate way. It's almost like a vampire society.

JE: *So we become vampires?*

KW: We become vampires, and we become victims of vampires. Our thought forms are the vampires as well as people.

JE: *The opposite of being leaky is saying, "I want; gimme."*

KW: If you are going to leak to somebody, there's got to be somebody on the other end taking. And it's a person or it's a system or a thought form or a group.

JE: *So vampirism is very active now?*

KW: In the modern western world—in a huge way.

JE: *I wonder if that's why our movies are so violent. Is the psyche of our culture being enacted?*

KW: The phenomenon has always been with us. We reflect what is going on within us, in our literature, in our storytelling—that's what storytelling is all about—that is one of its functions; it's other function is to introduce something new into a culture. For us, in this modern culture, the biggest storytelling is found on TV and in the movies—those are the big stage. Most of the people in this culture have their faces aimed at the television set and the movie screen.

JE: *What's your take on the children in the schools like the Columbine massacre and the outbreak of violence and depression among the young people in our culture?*

KW: In this cultural experiment that we have been involved in for thousands of years now, with each generation we have passed down this way of being and with each generation we have added more to it. We've found new ways, new possibilities, new probabilities; and it has become more extreme with every generation. We are now at the end of the wheel, and we are down to the most extreme. We are living out the last possibilities.

JE: *Is there anything parents can do, considering that we are all the parents of this generation? Is there anything in your wisdom tradition that contributes to how we can help recover the children?*

KW: The Hetakas always said, "it only takes one person to change the world." The most vital, the most important thing we can do for our children is to learn the truth of who we are as individuals, each of us, and to live the truth of who we really are. In that song, in that truth, without any judgments—about anything, is our point of connectedness to all things. Each Being is unique as an individual, and we are all connected. When we have a living experience of this connectedness and a living experience of who and what we are, we see the song-ness in everything else, we see the aliveness, we see this huge vast extraordinariness in everything. When we can experience that, we can't hurt the other or judge the other; we can't do things that involve power over. We can't believe in inequality, self-importance, self-aggrandizement—those things can't exist in us anymore. If we personally and individually learn to be our song and live it, we will teach by example to our young. Our children learn it by osmosis, by watching; and when they have it, they will live it, they will teach it to their children. Just the action of it, of living and feeling your own song, exploring with appreciation and awe the songs of everything else, what that radiates out into the world. The energy field that comes out of our song, the energy we leave behind—that teaches others; it teaches others all about a way of being, how to do it and how to be it. It changes us forever. That alone, teaches many, many people now and for generations to come. We can speak of being the truth of who we are, explore that uniqueness; and in exploring our connectedness, we teach that to the children. If we teach the techniques of how to explore it to our children, then they will live it and pass it on. Each person must take responsibility for themselves. What we think, feel and do is our legacy we are leaving behind. What are you choosing to leave behind?

One of my student-teachers has four kids—a ten year old, fourteen year old, sixteen year old, and a seventeen year old; the sixteen year old is deaf. Since she has been studying with me, she has made an extreme dedication to finding her song, learning it, living it, being it, unplugging all of those masks, waking up, and really exploring the depths of who she is and what medicine is. There is a lot that she can't verbally say to her kids. They have been too young and they're very acculturated in our modern society—interacting with their peers, going to school, watching TV. So what she says about this tradition and what she is learning has to come out in pieces and at times when they are asking and when they are curious; otherwise, they'll be modern kids and just turn away. So the most dramatic impact she can have is to live it—to be a living example. She's been extremely dedicated in doing this; and in these five years that I have been watching her and her kids, they are the ones that talk about the truth of themselves and being in their own song, living their truth, exploring their uniqueness, exploring their connectedness and the equality of all things. They have learned just by being with her and watching her. The oldest, the seventeen year old, was in my last first level class. Just before the class was to come about, he heard that it was happening and he told her, "I want to do this!"

The fourteen year old was having trouble sleeping so she gave him the CD with the Ceremony of finding your own song and told him to put it on repeat and fall to sleep with it. He had the best night's sleep he had ever had and continued to do this ceremony on his own initiative every night to go to sleep by. Not long after that, he asked her to teach him the other ceremonies too. From his direct experience and knowing he wrote this poem:

My Song

My Song, my own unique melody
The perfect rhythm, the perfect rhyme
A serene and silent reflection
Of the beauty that is my Soul

My Song, a personal piece of God
A symphony of images, a record of my life
The lessons that I learned, the wisdom I gained
The music of my memories

My Song, the lullaby of my feelings
The singing to sleep each night
Weaving a tale of calm and quiet existence
Of peaceful glades and open plains
Of unmoving mountains and endless forests

My Song, my own personal ballad
Of peace
Joy, happiness,
And wisdom

My Song
My Self

©*John Corff, 14 years old*

We do have an effect—so you can see: we are changing the world one person at a time, from the inside out. Each of us adding our piece to the building of a culture based on the positive turning wheel.

INTERVIEW WITH
DON ALBERTO TAZTO AND SILVIA REYNOSO

(translator and assistant)

March, 2001

Rumipampa, Ecuador, South America

JE: *Please describe soul loss in the Quechua culture, how you experience soul loss, and what it looks and feels like.*

AT/S: Firstly, it is part of the fifth element – known as the *jushai* or the *tchi-tchi*—part of the element which we call the "soul." The loss of the soul happens sometimes because of very strong fear. You could also lose your soul because the path you walk was not in harmony with you. It could also happen because somebody who knows how to make a "work" [witchcraft] can steal your soul. It also can be because a person is very weak, maybe you don't have the right way of life, not a good way of life, and you can lose your soul. It also happens because the way of living allows another force to come into your body and your soul.

JE: *Would that be like a possession?*

AT/S: Yes, it can be like a possession because the person allows that to happen.

JE: *Because the soul is not there, it leaves a space or an emptiness for another force to come in?*

AT/S: Not in all cases, just in that last case.

JE: *For example, say moving from community life or out here in the beauty and then moving into the city, would that possibly be a cause of soul loss?*

AT/S: It could happen when you are not ready for a change of life.

JE: *How do you experience soul loss when you are with someone? How do you sense that there is that loss?*

AT/S: Basically, the patient will have aches and pains, and they can make a personal kind of bed and find that nothing works. Another one is that the person doesn't feel like eating much and anything they eat they feel like throwing up. More frequently, it happens that they get scared about something, they don't want to eat, and they cry for everything, and they don't sleep well.

You could also realize when you are doing a healing on this person that the person needs to get all their elements together. Another case could be that this person doesn't follow a conversation; he kind of loses focus.

JE: *Can you see it in the eyes?*

AT/S: Usually the eyes will not have much shine.

JE: *Are there any other ways of noticing it?*

AT/S: If a person continually starts something and never finishes; he can't really focus on one thing.

JE: *Would it form a mental illness?*

AT/S: If, after a long time, they don't take care of it, it could produce a mental problem. It can also produce anemia.

JE: *Are there other symptoms?*

AT/S: Diarrhea is another symptom. When they don't have anything in their stomach and excrement is like the egg white that they are losing. They may also have another symptom which is a loss of sexual drive. It's like saying, "I love you but I don't want to be with you."

Jane Ely, Ph.D., D.Min.

JE: *In my culture, a lot of soul loss is in alcoholism, drug addiction, materialism. Would any of that also be in this culture?*

At/S: There are some cases, but not as many, because materially they don't have that much so they can't afford it.

JE: *Would alcohol also be a factor of soul loss in this culture?*

AT/S: For some of the people but not typically all. With the people that we work with, we haven't seen that much. But there are probably plenty in the city. Especially in the small communities, there isn't much drinking. There was alcoholism about twenty years ago but now it has stopped.

JE: *Is that because the traditional ways are being taught and are coming back to the community?*

AT/S: Yes, they also are realizing the consequences of alcoholism.

JE: *Is there a healing ceremony to find that fragmented soul energy and bring it back to the fifth element?*

AT/S   The strong herbs that we use, the sour herbs, and water to clear. That is the first part. Then you do an air cleansing, then an egg cleansing, and also pass the egg of a hen that has been fertilized, and pass a candle around. You pass it over everything. Then you use cold water.

JE: *You said pass a candle also, the same way as the egg?*

AT/S: The egg is on the skin. It is closed. It is a tradition that you hold an egg and as you pray you start passing it over the whole body. The egg will absorb everything. Also, the person should clean the diet. They should also abstain from sex for at least nine days.

JE: *So that is the whole process of the ceremony?*

AT/S: Because they have so many lamas, they also use the wool of the lama to pass over the person. And they also use the poop of the lama, the dried poop, for cleaning. In special cases, they use the urine of the lama and they wet the person with that.

SR: (*I was asking if maybe you could use a sheep instead of a lama but he says he doesn't know. For them the lama is very special, a sacred animal.*)

JE: *Are these all cleansing of the energies?*

AT/S: Yes, but it is not necessary that you do all of them. You could do one of them, depending on what you see the person needs.

JE: *Are there levels of soul loss—different strengths of soul loss? The more severe the soul loss the more medicine you would need to cleanse.*

AT/S: You also need more time and you may need to repeat some of the processes. You may also need to talk a lot to that person to make sure he or she understands that they need to heal. Many people, when they are very lost, do not understand that they need healing.

JE: *They don't even know that they are lost?*

AT/S: They don't know they are lost and they don't want to have a healing.

JE: *We were talking about the actual process of soul retrieval and the cleansing and we were beginning to get into the process of how the retrieval happens.*

AT/S: The main thing is to ask the great force of life to help harmonize that person, regardless of which technique you use. When you use the elements it would be good to ask before you do it - to mother wind - if you build a fire, to mother fire - when you blow the water on the person, to mother water - and to mother earth to help harmonize. This would be a ceremony that uses the four elements and the four directions. To complement that, you sing with the energy of the earth and the heavens. Then the *tchi-tchi* or the *jushai*, which is the soul of the person, will come back, which is our main energy. It feels like it is being called. You have to call it. After you harmonize the body, then you call. The call is: *shammu, shammu, shammu*, which means come, come, come, back.

JE: *Does the soul fragment then come back and join with the rest of the harmonized body?*

AT/S: Yes, depending on the retrieval and the situation of the patient that is also in harmony. You could do one treatment and it would be enough, or it could take several treatments.

JE: *Is there a change in behavior immediately or does it take time for integration?*

AT/S: You will see the changes in minutes if it is finished. If it is not finished, if they need further treatment, then you will see no change.

JE: *Would you recommend that they come back within a certain period of time?*

AT/S: It could be next day or next week, depending on how the patient is reacting. If there is a favorable reaction, then you wait a week until the next treatment. If there is no change at all, then you would do it the next day.

JE: *Is there anything you recommend a patient do to bring the consciousness to themselves, to bring the awakening to themselves?*

AT/S: The person should smell the flowers, or petals of flowers. Also they should not eat any animal meat and cannot have sex. If it is a child you are working with, you put your left hand on the base of the neck and the right hand on the coccyx and you hold the baby upside down and you shake him or her and call the soul. They are facing down. If you can push with your hand on the stomach area a little bit, then that would be good because that child may have diarrhea. The baby is facing up, the head is down but the baby is looking at you. So you hold him first, holding the neck and the coccyx, and then you support the baby on your legs and push their stomach a little bit, and call at the same time. In our culture, we make the call *shammu, shammu,* and we call the soul back.

JE: *Do you actually experience the moment, as the caller, when the soul part comes home?*

AT/S: Yes, you can feel it and the patient also can feel it. The patient feels better and you can see that he is looking better—the face is more mellow.

JE: *Is there anything else we should know about this method?*

AT/S: When there is not harmony in a person's life, any kind of negative energy is not good for your soul. When there is harmony in your life, it is very hard to lose your soul because you are full of life. It is always good to look for things that will bring harmony into your life.

JE: *Can you speak a little bit about the five elements -- earth, air, fire, water – and   the fifth one?*

AT/S: It is *jushai*.   It is the result of the four elements being in balance. We have a soul and we have a spirit. The spirit would be the *jushai*.   But it is not only the spirit, it is the soul, the spirit and ourself - the essence of ourself. When we leave our body, for example, our soul stays here because our soul is of this world and, until our body completely decomposes, that soul, that energy which is here with our body right now is going to stay here. Our spirit goes out and keeps on working and learning. It is the infinite one. The essence of who we are, ourself, goes too. The *jushai* is all that - our spirit, our soul, our essence - it is all together. When all the elements are in balance in the body, then the *jushai* grows. The soul is like the aura of the person but the *jushai* is more than that, it is the cosmos energy which never dies. It will continue as our spirit and our essence of who we are. So that is the fifth element. It varies in people, how big or how small they have it, depending on how balanced the elements are in a person's life.

JE: *Thank you very much.*

INTERVIEW WITH
LUISAH TEISH

Oakland, California

June 14, 2001

L.T: For the past twenty years I have been what is called a "Mother of the Spirits". That allows me to do a certain level of spiritual work with people. It has included everything from listening to the baby in the belly to different rites of passage, conducting ceremonies, doing funerals and other rituals. Now I have graduated to what is called *Iyanifa* which means Mother of Destiny [in African culture]. As a Mother of Destiny, there is a high level of knowledge that I have to achieve. My elder has told me that I have to memorize thirty-two verses of our sacred oracle by the end of August. I have to memorize them in English, so that is like a verse a day. I do not speak Yoruba fluently. I play and sing in Yoruba, so there is the issue of really coming away from a superficial understanding of it to understanding the language and its cultural concepts that go with it. This is definitely a period of intellectual and spiritual growth for me because that is what my Nigerian elders require. They require it in songs, dances and prayers, this kind of thing, so I think any gaps in my knowledge about the spiritual culture are about to be filled.

I am really like a bridge across cultures. That is one of the things that is a life assignment for me and one of the things of which I am proud, that I have been allowed to participate in enough different cultures that I can bring understanding about what is going on. My best example of it is not around spiritual teachings but what we think of as a very mundane thing.

LT: I went into a Chinese fast food place and there was an African man standing there with the Chinese cook and they were screaming at each other. The cook was pounding on the table. I said to the African man, "What's the problem, brother?" He said, "I don't understand why I cannot make this man to give me some real food." I turned to the cook and said, "What's happening, cook?" He said, "No matter what I give him he is not satisfied with what I have fixed." I know in the Bay area that Chinese cooks will really try to put together anything that you ask for. They are not stuck on their menu. I've gone and said that I didn't really want this, can you do me some of that. So I said, "Wait a minute and see if I can help." I asked the African, "Do you want chicken or fish?" He said, "Chicken." I said, "Do you want ground nut chop or pepe soup?" He said, "I want ground nut chop." I said, "Okay, do you want fou-fou or yellow rice?" He said, " I want yellow rice." I turned to the cook and said, "Give this man some yellow chicken curry over rice with vegetables over the vegetable fried rice and a few pieces of fried chicken on top." The cook went in, fixed it, laid it down in front of the African, and the African said, "Now this is food!"

So I translated it. I am able to do the same with spiritual concepts and cultural practices. The work that I am about to do now will make me even better able to do that, as well as take me deeper into my own spiritual development.

JE: *Will you be going back to Haiti or Nigeria to do that?*

LT: I have to go to both and that is one of the things I am worried about right now. I am supposed to go to Nigeria in August to deliver a paper on contemporary interpretations. But, you know, you get these notices from the bank telling you that you have no money! I am waiting to hear from my Haitian elder because she wants me to go to Haiti in September. Because I am a kind of cultural attache, traveling around a lot is part of my path. I don't know, the way it looks now. If I follow the schedule I'm supposed to follow, it would be Nigeria in August, Haiti in September, New Orleans in October, Benin in November, Mexico in December and Brazil in February. That's a bit much. I need to stretch some of that out. In between, I am moving and revamping my library in a smaller house and it's hard on the body.

JE: *I sent you some information on my book project. I'm not sure if you have had a chance to look at it. I thought I would refresh your memory and bring you up-to-date on the topic. My book is called "Remembering the Ancestral Soul" and it is about soul loss and recovery. I am very interested in looking at the original background of indigenous cultures and North American indigenous traditions in cross-cultural perspectives. As part of this exploration, I am curious about African-American views on soul loss. And how the African indigenous practices can help bring people home*

LT: Well, you didn't bite off much, did you?

JE: *I feel as if this is going to be a lifelong project!*

LT: I'm glad you know that because you're going to need a lot of patience. You are asking to excavate our ancient healing methods and test them on some illness which has gone to a new dimension. Know what I'm talking about?

JE:. *Absolutely. To help us focus, I am asking if there is the concept of soul loss in the Yoruba way. How do you identify it? How do you view it?*

LT: The first problem we have is that I am going to sit here and try to talk in a linear fashion about a spiral. And then, because we are talking in English, almost everything I say would have to be qualified by Yoruba concepts. In order to answer your question, I am going to have to talk about a concept called Ori. When Ori is translated into English, it translates as "the head". As soon as I say a person's "head," the Western person sees a neck and then this circular oval thing that is sitting on top of that neck, which is sort of disconnected from the rest of the body and certainly does not extend into any other dimensions. We don't mean that at all, okay?

When I talk about Ori then I will have to talk about Ifa which is one's destiny. Unfortunately, most of the time in the west, destiny has some kind of negative thing about it, as if there's a biological determinism or social Darwinism. Unfortunately, I have the job of starting this answer out with negatives. What I want to do is try to explain what happens to me when you ask the question.

First of all, we function in Yoruba tradition and in most of the traditions that have come out of the mixture of people of West African descent, and the native peoples of this hemisphere, under a European overlay. That is the first thing you have to understand. When people were brought to this hemisphere and changed, absolutely involuntarily, long before Columbus, there was interaction between what we now call Mezo-American, South America. Then we came and changed. There was a meeting of indigenous traditions, an exchange of information between the Africans and the Indians, especially around the herbs of this land and those that we had smuggled in under our tongues and in our hair, that kind of thing.

There were similar notions of inspirited nature so that we knew the trees and the animals and the elephants talked and interacted, were receptive and responsive. In both cases, the indigenous people of this hemisphere and the indigenous people who came from the Mother Continent, Africa, were both laboring under the thought of disembodied concepts of the Christian church. So we developed traditions that were a camouflage. It was illegal to practice our own traditions. The Catholic church pretty much sponsored the slave trade, so people were being made Christian Catholics left and right. What we did was identify our deities with the Catholic saints in a lot of cases. That is how the traditions went on, as evidenced in the Caribbean Islands, throughout South America, parts of the United States, especially New Orleans and other similar cities.

There was a synchronization that happened, or a polyglot, where a number of elements, together with some of the original concepts, got stained by a disembodied way of being, but it never fully penetrated us.

To get back to your question. There is the impact of having to hold onto one's cultural soul under the face of oppression. We have done that through the music and dance, the food and tonality of language. We have held on to as much of that as we possibly could.

Interestingly enough, our music is called soul music, our food is called soul food, because we know that is where the collective soul has been kept together. We know this.

Getting more into the soul of a community, you know, because we come out of a tradition of an extended family - all the positivism, all the negativism - there is a sense of "us" that maintains a soul. We are discussing this now in my class because we are doing African-American rituals and there are only two African-Americans in the class - myself and another woman. So, having to explain to Anglo-Americans how we see ourselves, how we see others, and how we see others looking at us, there is a sense of kinship. I can walk into a room where there are fifty people and yet there are two black people and we automatically feel related to each other, not because we know anything about each other, except that we are black and have shared the same historical experience. It is only through maintaining that kind of kinship that we have been able to hold onto the soul. That is the only way we have been able to do it.

Now, when you get down to the individual person, knowing that every family, every extended family, every community, every nation, is made up of inter-related individuals, we can begin to talk about individual and collective destiny and my part in that whole thing. There is a concept in Ori and the idea is that this head which is sitting on my shoulders is something my spirit chose when I decided to take a body. In my mother's womb I chose to be, to do, and to have certain things in this life. I determined to be born black and female at this point in time, to this particular set of parents, in order to have these experiences, do this work, and receive this direction.

We would say that this is my head that I brought to earth, but I have a head in heaven. Heaven is not that place where the streets are paved with gold and we're sucking on honey. We are not into that at all. Neither is our heaven somewhere where you just go and hang out. There is work being done over there; there is interaction with us here; we come and go in and out of there - that's what I'm saying. We say the world is the marketplace, but heaven is going home. You go home, you rest for awhile, and then you go back to the marketplace.

So I have come here. I made a contract with Creation before I arrived. The first encounter that I have is the act of birth. As I turn to come through the birth canal, because of the energy I am exerting to be born, there is some memory loss.

Then I hit this air, with this light, with the people who are around me. If they don't handle things right, we have some more loss. In my family, we sing to the child in the womb, we massage the belly, we coax the baby out, saying, "You need to know that you are welcome. Come on now, we are waiting on you, you agreed to come." When that baby's head crowns we sing a welcome song. There are rituals all the way through to let this child know we expected it. "You agreed to come to us. Come on, let's get on with what you came here to do." So there are bits of loss of who we agreed to be. When that child is exposed to the large world into what we call socialization, unless the extended family is very careful, there can be more loss.

Out here in this world, we are interacting with a lot of other people who have forgotten just about everything, who have forgotten that they should have a sacred relationship with nature, who have forgotten that we are supposed to have a mutually helpful relationship to each other, and who have forgotten our intimate connection to the spirit. If you come into too much contact with too many of these, you are exposed to physical, mental, emotional and spiritual pollutants.

That is where a person like me comes in. I am trained to identify conditions of soul loss, or being off one's path, or having forgotten who you came here to be. I am trained at how to take a look at that and how to re-balance the energies to get you back on track.

This is what all our rituals are about, getting you back in alignment with your sacred self and with nature, community and spirit. That's what all of it is about. Hopefully and theoretically, I have been doing pretty good for the last twenty years, but the studies that I am going into now will make it easier and better. Actually, it should put me in a position where, when I am finished with these studies, I will be better able to train people who are in the position I am in now, and to be more efficient in this work. We have what we call "cleaning and feeding the head" so that you can remember. The three things we do are talk, clean and feed. We have to communicate with spirit and with each other to find out what is off center.

Then we have the job of cleaning up the pollutants that have occurred and then feeding, making us strong so that we can get back on our road. If you can think of someone who is on the road of life who has a traumatic experience - let's say they stumble on a big rock, they fall in the dirt and sort of forget where they were going. The journey has been long, they have had nothing to eat, so they stumble up to my house. I bring them in and ask them where they came from. They only have piecemeal information. I examine them and find a piece of a map. I pull out the map and recognize that map. That is what my divination does. It lays out a map of the way you are supposed to be going, where you are coming from, where you are right now.

So I say, "Come, come in. Let me take you to the bathroom and give you a bath. I've got some clothes over here that might fit you. Here, eat some of this and, by the way, the road you want to be on is right here. Head on back out."

If you take that analogy of the individual and begin to apply it to families, communities, nations, the planet, then you have to deal with Luisah's nightmare. At times I have had arguments with the Creator. I have said, "Creator, I bet you made a mistake. I think you made a mistake." It just seems to me that human beings shouldn't be able to kill each other. We shouldn't have the power to destroy the water. Who do we think we are?

We have a folk tale, we have myths, that are supposed to help us out. One of our myths says that the one who created human beings started out making a batch of people who were kind, intelligent and beautiful. Then the Creator was so proud He tapped a jug of wine and the next ones He created were kind and intelligent but not so pretty. He drank some more, made some not intelligent or pretty but kind. Then He got so drunk that a bunch of mean-spirited ones were created, and got so drunk that He fell asleep.

JE: *Was it God, the Creator?*

LT: Not the ultimate (Olodumare) but the one who shapes a child in the womb (Obatala). He fell asleep and, upon awakening,

He found these creatures were biting each other, about to destroy everything. He thought to destroy everything in response to that but saw that some of the ones who were intelligent were helping some of those who were kind, and some of the ones who were kind were helping some of the ones who were ugly. So He said, "Let them work it out. I won't destroy everything." And that's why we have all these others come in to help us work it out.

I went through a period where I feared and asked the Creator, "How drunk did You get? And how much of a mess are we going to be allowed to make here?" What came back was, "Whatever you don't like about what is going on on earth, you fix it." And so I used to have this recurring dream where I was looking at myself through the lens of a camera. At first, all I could see was me shaking. Then the lens would open wider and I could see me on my knees, and then the lens would open wider and there was a brush in my hand, and it would open wider. What I finally saw was me, on my knees, scrubbing the world with a toothbrush. That is Luisah's nightmare. One of the things that I do when I am traveling around all over the world is to find out how many of us have tooth-brushes, and how much scrubbing is going on, and where can I get together and help scrub. That's where I'm at.

JE: *That is a powerful image and a good one to be reminded of.*

LT: Thank you. You identify, huh? It's good to know that we're not alone. Sometimes all you have to do is turn on the 10 o'clock news.

JE: *What has recently been bothering me is my level of despair for the world. Part of this whole grappling is the fear of losing the soul, losing the remembering, losing the lineage, losing the ancestry, our history. It is almost like trying to stop a runaway train wreck. My level of investigation and personal experiences has really brought me to a new depth.*

LT: Back in the 80's, I was at a women's encampment - it was a summer thing. You know the way a lot of things are supposed to be spiritual and how they get done. In this particular instance there were two things that happened that I want to talk about. On the opening day, the person who had organized it and gathered all the teachers together said, "Okay, we are going to sit in this circle and I want you to slap your hands on your knees, snap your fingers and stomp your feet and make this sound." I said, "What are we doing?" And she said, "We are doing a Native American rain chant." I said, "Excuse me. We have 280 women here who are about to camp out. Do we want it to rain?" And she said, "No, of course not." So I said, "Then why are we doing a rain chant?" And she said, "I don't really believe it is going to rain."

JE: *Was she a Native American?*

LT: No! In that moment, the gap between where I was and where she was was humongous. There are all kind of issues about respect and understanding and how to use words and what you do with them.

JE: *And the power behind the words and the power behind the incantation....*

LT: Absolutely. It's like, I'm not whistling Dixie here and I am certainly not going to show disrespect to Native American spirits by calling them for nothing. That is what is happening all the time.

That takes me into a certain kind of despair, when I'm trying to do this kind of work.

At this same event, there was this methodology that they wanted us to use. Supposedly, what we were going to do was that every woman would take twenty minutes to tell her story and the other women would sit silently in the circle and not say anything, not touch her, not do anything except sit there. And I said, "I'm not going to do it. I'm sorry, I'm not going to do it because I have to bottle up my intuition. If this woman is telling me something and spirit tells me she needs to be touched, I am going to touch her. If spirit tells me to go get such-and-such an herb, I am going to get it. If spirit tells me to sing such-and-such a song, I am going to sing it. I cannot do this." So I did not participate in that. Later on, after that first session, a woman came to me. I am known for being able to set up house anywhere, so I had taken over this utility shed and turned it into a studio apartment. The woman came to the apartment and she was crying her eyes out. When I asked her what the matter was she said, "You know, I was in a group yesterday and all the women were talking about their babies and their pregnancies and their sex lives. I recently had a hysterectomy and all I could feel was this great, big hole in me." So I started telling her stories about Yemaya, the Goddess of the Ocean, and how this ocean is this big pregnant belly with all these fish floating around. I gave her a visualization where I had her go down to the bottom of the ocean and see a castle made of sponge in the distance, go knock on the door, and here comes a black-skinned mermaid with green seaweed hair and dark angular breasts who invites you in. I wove this whole story for her which is out of our mythology, until she fell asleep. She spent the night at my place and when we woke up in the morning she was just gleaming. She said, "Oh, Teish, I had this wonderful dream. I had this great big belly full of salt water and there were all these little fish floating around and they were all my children and I talked to them." That's medicine.

I can't have somebody dictating some dry methodology to me when I know what the medicine is. My pet peeve, and one of the things I am trying to deal with, one of the problems in our culture, is that issues of racism and sexism and classism and all the other "isms" are not being effectively addressed because people leave the spiritual component out of it. There are four directions, minimally. We can get into six and eight and sixteen, but minimally four with a decent center. Whenever the spiritual component is left out we are just whistling in the wind.

There are times when I have had to be sort of reprimanded by my elders for hiding in the bushes. I will go into the woods and I won't come out. There have been times when they have said, "There is work for you to do." And I have said, "Unh, unh, I am in the bushes right now. I don't want to come out."

When I travel and go somewhere, I have to go through the local rain forest; I've got to be on the outskirts in the countryside. Sometimes when things get crazy, then I'll go over to the Home Depot and pull up a chair in the garden section and just sit there. If I don't, there's a strange kind of violence that comes over me. It is that place where the Goddess would rather destroy me, and Her I have to watch.

JE: *It reminds me of the Hindu tradition - Durga who is the builder up and Kali Ma who is the destroyer. We have both those sides in us.*

LT: That's amazing because, when I was in Borneo the Spring of last year, there is a temple in a place called Kotayinabalu. I did not go up into the temple because you had to climb over 200 steps to get there, but there were shrines with offerings down below. My friend went up. I was dressed all in white, standing in front of the temple waiting for my friend, when this East Indian man walked by with his son. He looked at me and he said, "Kali Ma!"

June 15, 2001

Soquel, California

JE: *How do you recognize soul loss? How have you been trained in this healing way?*

PW: While I do have Apache and Comanche and also some native from Mexico in my heritage, my training does not come from any tribal tradition.

JE: *Describe how the training came to you.*

PW: In the beginning, the training came through several experiences of awakening to my Native American heritage. One of my first teachers was Barbara Brennan, the founder of the Barbara Brennan School of Healing. In the first workshop I took with her, she had an evening of drumming and movement. As soon as I heard the drumming, I went into an altered state and started chanting and dancing in a very traditional Native American way. Later, at another time, I met a man who made and sold Native American flutes in Southern California. When I first heard the sound of the flute as he played it, I started to cry—it touched a deep place in my heart of remembering. Sometime later I went to Sedona with a friend where we took a tour of the area with an indigenous man. He took us to one of the power spots where there was a medicine wheel and, on the way there, he played some music that was sung in the traditional Cherokee language. I started to cry as soon as I heard it; and when we got to the land where the medicine wheel was, I broke down in tears again just remembering my people's way.

It has been a path of remembering. I have always been guided not to follow one particular Native teaching, but to awaken to the shaman within me. The focus for the last fifteen years has been on my own awakening. Through the process of self- healing, my own Native or shamanic nature has just come forth.

JE: *Your way is a visionary way of doing it, more like the awakening of a mystic?*

PW: It's the only way I know. I remember one day in Monterey, the Nature spirits all started to talk to me at once—it was sort of frightening. Everything just started talking. At first I was scared and I tried to get away from it but it just wouldn't stop. Everything was talking—the trees, the birds, the ocean, the wind—and finally I started to commune with them. I remember sitting on the ground and putting my belly to the Earth, forming a deep, deep connection to Mother Earth and experiencing my love for her. She came alive for me in that moment and I became her child. Surrendering to Mother Earth was very easy; I felt very little resistance.

Where I experienced more resistance was in surrendering to Great Spirit. Through my personal process work, I discovered I had created a split within myself, associating Mother Earth with the lower charkas (the way of my people) and Great Spirit with the upper charkas (the way of the white man). Healing this split was an important key in allowing my healership to unfold.

JE: *Do you feel you've been doing your own soul recovery? How does that happen for you?*

PW: Yes, I have spent the last sixteen years slowly recovering from soul loss. At times I have been very conscious of my soul retrieval, setting my intention through ceremonies and vision quests. Other times, it has just happened through my personal process.

JE: *How do you recognize when there has been some form of recovery within yourself?*

PW: I've recognized it in different ways. One time after doing a ceremony I woke up the next morning feeling something was different; I felt more whole. I stared into the mirror and did not recognize who I was looking at. There was somebody in the mirror looking at me then who hadn't been there before. At other times I have recognized it through having more vitality or energy present; or through my speech—my ability to be articulate and converse— which had always been very difficult for me. In addition, I have at times recognized the recovery of a fragment through smell, sight; or physically through a sense of being present. I remember not too long ago, I felt like an adult for the first time in my life. I felt very deeply then that more of me was adult than child. So it has been through an increased ability to be more present in my daily life which indicates to me that I am more here.

JE: *Does the practice of being with your pipe every day, which is part of your spiritual practice, help you?*

PW: It used to. I gave up my pipe when I was in New Mexico last December. I ran across four rattlesnakes and gave them the offering of the pipe. It was a very powerful ceremony. So I no longer do that ritual, but it served me for about 10 years as a powerful way of committing to the path and connecting to Mother Earth and Great Spirit. Everyone needs some kind of daily ritual.

JE: *How do you recognize the symptoms of soul loss?*

PW: Sometimes I see the aspect floating above them or the place in space where it has gone. I get a sense of it or a picture. Sometimes I hear an absence in the person's voice. I'm very kinesthetic so I feel it too. I feel like they are not all there; something's missing. Often in their sharing, people will, without knowing it, actually speak of what is missing through the words they choose. I have also heard the cries of the lost soul parts.

JE: *You've heard the cries not only of individuals but also of the Earth in her soul loss?*

PW: Yes, I have also heard the cries of Mother Earth. This has been an important piece of my development as a healer: the ability to keep my heart open and stay present when I'm hearing the cries of lost souls.

JE: *And how do you work with the person once you recognize soul loss?*

PW: The form the soul retrieval takes depends on the client. I have several methods and I try to use the one that best fits the client. In some ways I feel like I'm a shape shifter: I'm trained as a Core Energetics therapist, an energy practitioner, and also use my natural shamanic gifts. The soul retrieval can be very therapeutic or it can be very shamanic. The mode depends on the client and what they need me to be for them.

JE: *Can you describe how the work differs—first the therapeutic approach and then the shamanic approach?*

PW: Therapeutically, it is closely resembles a traditional therapy session—sitting on the couch and talking. I may offer a guided meditation since some people are more comfortable with that.

Pounding the drum might scare some people, so I do not use the drum; I use my voice instead. I might begin with a John Bradshaw technique such as working with the inner child by having the client talk about a young aspect of themselves and then have them roll back in time to connect and feel this part of themself.

JE: *Once you get them into that state, what happens?*

PW: I believe that an aspect of our soul leaves because the person could not withstand whatever trauma occurred. So the aspect that carries the trauma separates from the larger consciousness of the individual. The individual could not do whatever needed to be done, could not say whatever needed to be said, or could not feel whatever needed to be felt. So I aid the client in discovering and connecting to this part of them. Then we create a safe environment to release the trauma. In my practice as a Core Energetics therapist, sometimes I use body movement or role-playing. For example, I place a pillow on a chair, symbolizing the mother, and have the client say something to her—something that they were never able to say before. Sometimes a client needs to move the body to release held trauma; or they may need to release painful emotions they have not felt safe to feel.

JE: *You were talking about clients being actively involved— physically, mentally, and emotionally. How do you support the client in bringing that soul part into the present now?*

PW: After the client has released the trauma, I aid them in integrating this lost aspect by learning to hold this part of their self in a new way. I would say that the difference between the therapeutic and shamanic modes is that the client's mind is more active in the therapeutic modality. But there's a fine line here—it's a real dance not to let the mind control the process completely.

JE: *Do you find in that situation that it might not happen because the ego gets involved?*

PW: It can be more difficult, especially if you have somebody who is very intellectual. That's the difficulty in the traditional therapeutic modality. You have to be careful - since the client is usually sitting up, the mind is often in control. It's a dance to try to get them into a surrendered, altered state while still allowing their mind to be part of the process. And for some people, it just will not work. I then suggest they lie down and I take them on a journey using my drum to get the mind out of the way. For some people, the mind will not allow the process to happen.

JE: *And so then you would choose the more shamanic approach?*

PW: Right, if they are open to it.

JE: *And can you describe your shamanic approach for soul retrieval?.*

PW: Well, most of my soul retrievals have been done in a two-day workshop format. I have taken my therapeutic work and combined it with shamanism. I have the participants bring a picture of themselves at whatever age they feel guided to. We create an altar on which we place the pictures and do a ceremony. Then I take the group on a shamanic journey to meet their power animal which guides them to their lost soul part. I also have them walk in nature and bring back an object that represents their lost soul part.

The first day is spent connecting to this lost aspect of soul that is ready to be retrieved and discovering what they need to do to bring it back. They are taking a more active role than they would with a traditional shaman who lies down next to the person and does most of the work. They are part of the process.

The second day, I give them an opportunity in ceremony with the whole group to express an act of power, feel or say something they have never allowed themselves to do. This is done to aid in the soul retrieval by building the participants' courage and strength so they will be able to hold the lost aspect of their self when it has been brought back.

Then I end with a more traditional soul retrieval. I call in the Four Directions and the ancestors, and I have my assistant do the drumming. All the participants lie down with enough room for me to kneel next to them. As the drum beats, I go to each person; I have my eagle feather, my rattle, and my power objects with me. Often when I am doing this, the lost part of them is already hovering right there over them, so there is not a lot of effort on my part. It depends on the person. Sometimes everything is ready, and all it takes is rattling and using the wind to blow that part of them in. I retrieve and blow the lost soul right into their heart. Then, for others, there is still some trauma that needs to be released from their energy field first. I will aid them in expressing this trauma. In this case, I might then need to journey to the underworld to recover the lost soul. I find allowing them to be involved creates a very powerful experience; I believe it supports the integration so that each person is able to fully embody the soul retrieval.

There is a case I want to share with you. A participant came to my workshop who was very fragmented. All I could see above her were many fragmented pieces of her soul. I remember feeling, "Oh, my God, what am I going to do?" Finally, what came to me was to use a lasso like a cowboy would use. The best I could do was sort of round up all those pieces in a rope and bring them all together in one pile. Then I attached the end of the rope, the cord, into her third chakra. It was the best that could happen - at least the fragments then had a container to be within her.

JE: *And did you notice after that that your work with her shifted?*

PW: She became stronger. In fact, she did so well that she was able to take a break in our work together. Then she came back a year later and did another workshop. There had been a big shift for her - she was able to hold her fragmentation better- but longed for more wholeness. When I did her second soul retrieval, her fragmented soul had integrated and I was able to bring a part of her home. She was able to experience this during the retrieval and felt a large part of herself come in.

JE: *Do you follow up post-soul work to find out what their integration process is afterwards?*

PW: If they become my clients, I do. Usually, but not always, many of those who take the workshop will get back to me.

One man came because he had always made sounds at night-- kind of crying sounds. Over the years, these crying sounds had gotten so bad that his wife could no longer sleep with him at night. In the workshop he connected to a part of himself that was still sitting on the steps crying outside his childhood home, waiting for his father to come back. His parents had divorced and his father had left home, and he remembered how he would sit for hours crying, still waiting for Daddy. So in the workshop, he did a process in which he was able to feel and express the tears and pain of that child. His retrieval then was easy; the boy's soul was ready to come home and I brought him in. Later he got back to me and said that the night crying had stopped.

JE: *Do you ever request specific post-soul retrieval integration practices for a client?*

PW: Yes. After the soul retrieval, we take time to talk about integration. I encourage them to walk their act of power in their daily life. I explain how important it is for them to connect to the new part of them they have retrieved. They may need to change something in their life to keep this part from leaving again. They need to walk a new way and they may need practice to help them walk that new way.

I also tell them to be very careful with whom they share their journey. In the weeks following the workshop it's important that they stay quiet and let the integration happen, and not tell the story to someone who may not believe it or accept it. Even to be careful about who they spend time with (for example, not to be with disturbing people). Post-soul retrieval is really a re-birthing time.

JE: *How do you see soul loss in the larger context of our culture?*

PW: It really hurts my heart, because I see it all the time; it is difficult for me to see such profound forgetting in the world.

JE: *How do you work with your own despair when you see such huge soul loss around us?*

PW: I let myself feel it—just feel it even if tears have to come to keep my heart open. I'll often give healings to strangers I see throughout the day who are in deep soul loss by sending them love with prayers to awaken.

Once I was coming back from a vision quest and on the way back, I stopped at a store with a friend. There was this sharp, red car parked outside. The driver, a man in his twenties, had his hair perfectly done, spiked up, and was wearing perfect sunglasses. He had his look down; his mask was sharp. I saw him and my heart started hurting. I felt him and there was nothing inside. It was empty, Jane, such emptiness underneath. There was only this façade he had created. And I wondered, what would he do when he starts to lose the looks? When he hits his forties and fifties, what's life going to be like for him? I see such profound forgetting of the truth of who people really are and such a profound disconnection from the Earth.

To answer your question, I focus on the beauty and light that is here in all of us to the best of my ability. I try to serve humanity by allowing my own light to come forth. At times, the pain of our forgetting is too much for my heart and then I must allow the cleansing of tears.

JE: *One of the things I am exploring, Whitebuffalo, is the extent of soul loss in our society. Can you share your insights on how to turn this epidemic around? .*

PW: One of the ways I work with this is through my one-on-one private practice and my workshops. From a larger perspective, one of my visions is to create a non-profit organization to fund groups of healers to go to areas on the Earth that need cleansing from the pain we have left in the soil of the Earth—from the wars, from disasters, from all the things that have happened on the Earth. Mother Earth needs to be cleansed of what man has left behind.

JE: *What of our emotional and physical toxins and spiritual toxins?*

PW: Yes. So I see one way to have a bigger effect would be to really work on the Earth, to work with clearing and cleansing all the negative thought forms that have been left on the Earth. Going to particular sites, such as Gettysburg and some of the places where the massacres of Native Americans took place. Also in Europe there are many sites that need this work especially in Germany. And in doing so, what I'm hoping will happen is that the consciousness of that area, of that nation would then rise and help the consciousness of the people who inhabit it. I believe it would have a profound effect.

JE: *For example, a group going to the concentration camps and working with the lost souls there?*

PW: Yes! It's not just our emotional debris and negative thought forms. There are also all the lost souls who are caught between worlds, still walking the Earth on these sites. We as a community of healers and shamans need to come together and create a gateway to guide them home.

JE: *There is a form of Buddhist practice known as Tonglen that transforms dark, psychic residue to light and to source.*

PW: That sounds great—exactly the work I'm talking about. I have so much passion about this work. It will take well-trained healers who are able to hold both worlds without going into their own personal process to be able to do this level of work.

JE: *Do you become the bridge between the worlds?.*

PW: Yes, you are the bridge and as the bridge you must not get lost. This would be the challenge: to not allow your ego to get involved in the work. I had an experience of this at Joshua Tree National Park in California. During a pipe ceremony, a tribe of Native Americans came to me in the spirit world. They had been massacred by soldiers and were walking the land lost in pain. This was difficult for me to see and not react to what I was seeing. I talked to them and said it was time for them to go home but they seemed to have difficulty letting go of the trauma of their experience. As I was working with them, a group of soldiers also came in asking for help to go home. Using my pipe I created a ceremony for both parties to come together in peace and forgiveness. I was able to hold both groups so a healing could occur that would allow them all to return home. My challenge was not to allow my personal pain and the loss of my ancestors to interfere with the healing. It's difficult, when we are living in our toxic debris, to make a major shift of consciousness. The lifting and clearing of that debris and the releasing of these lost souls would allow a global shift in consciousness. But until that happens, it will be very difficult.

JE: *Would you comment on how it feels to be "soul-full"?*

PW: My father worked for the Ford Motor Company and was really into cars. When I was a child, he would always say you want to purchase an eight-cylinder engine, that they were the most powerful. Using the automobile as a metaphor, you could say we all have eight cylinder engines, yet many of us are running on only two. I see soul retrieval as gaining back a cylinder at a time so that we can all become eight-cylinder engines once again. That's how my own process feels to me; I retrieved all my cylinders and I just feel so much more full and alive. It's incredible! I couldn't imagine not taking this journey.

We must also remember that there are many ways to do soul retrieval. Practitioners should work in whatever form they are guided to use and feel comfortable with. Never feel that there's only one way. What is important is to find your own way and come forth with that.

INTERVIEW WITH
ANITA BARROWS

June 17, 2001

Berkeley, California

JE: *I would like to explore your perspective as therapist and mystical poet on the subject of soul loss and recovery. Would you begin by outlining your training and background?*

AB: I was the granddaughter of two rabbis. In my childhood, I practiced Judaism until I was about sixteen, at which point I left and sort of evolved for myself a kind of nature spirituality. In my adulthood I became a Catholic, converting in my early thirties, through reading Italian medieval poetry, Dante particularly, but others as well. I still go for the Eucharist now and again but practice is mostly Buddhism. That is one thread of my life.

I have written poetry ever since I was about six. My training, academically, was originally in English Literature. Then I got a Masters in English in Comparative Literature. I was on my way to a doctorate in Comparative Literature—French, German, English and Italian—until I decided just to take a Masters in Italian and leave. I taught in the Italian department at U.C. Berkeley for awhile, and then I got a Ph.D. in Psychology. It's a long road, many turns and changes.

JE: *When did you become a Buddhist?*

AB: In my twenties. I had always done some kind of contemplative, meditative practice. By the time I hit my late thirties, Buddhism was a practice more than a religion, a practice I could use to widen my attention and focus on the world. I felt very much that what I needed to do was to pay attention to the suffering, and Buddhism seemed a very good way to do it.

JE: *Can you describe how you see loss of soul?*

AB: I will give you an example. I was working with a female patient, who has an autistic child and is going through a number of difficulties in her marriage. She is now in the process of divorce and quite disoriented in many ways. What she has been doing to shore herself up amounts to compulsive eating and compulsive buying. She spends hours a day on the internet, ordering things that she doesn't need. She is spending her entire inheritance which are the funds she needs to get out of the marriage. I think she is an example of what our culture does to rob people of their souls.

I think that soul loss can happen in a number of ways. One is that we are disconnected from our roots. We are disconnected from our home. We are disconnected from belonging to one another in spirit and other living beings. What fills in that empty place in our capitalistic society is consumerism. That's fine for the powers-that-be because that is what keeps the wheels turning, but I think that we are all really disconnected. I see it in kids as well. I see that same pattern—acquiring, boredom, the inability to turn inward or to look out at nature—that is one route for soul loss.

Another (very connected) route is in the kinds of physical, emotional, and sexual abuses that goes on. The perpetrators of abuse are disconnected from their lives and so they are acting out a means of violence. I see so many kids in families who are not looked at for who they are. The parents have narcissistic needs that they impose on the kids, so very early on the kids lose track of their souls. It is stunning and terrifying. Kids are not being given anything by the schools or by the culture at large to grow on. We have wasted our children, and I see it. I have a 17-year-old who basically has dropped out of school. She's doing independent study. It is great for her because she can do it on her own and do her music and her art and the other things that she cares about. She was just dying in high school. She was exhausted all the time, drained by the lack of respect, the lack of stimulation, the lack of inspiration, the lack of nourishment.

JE: *So are the symptoms of soul loss all around us?*

AB: Yes, all around us. I think we could just keep going on about this subject forever.

JE: *I am very interested in your views on ways of re-vitalizing ourselves, bringing our souls home.*

AB: I think the union model, especially, is a way home. What I look at with my adult patients and some of the adolescents is dreams. The dream is a manifestation of the soul; the dream comes from a place that we can't determine, and we can't control. The dream tells us things we sometimes don't remember, things that we don't necessarily think about in our conscious lives. Through looking at dreams, people really do begin to change at very deep levels and reach into something inside themselves that they have lost.

A person comes to therapy because they have lost something. Very often, first dreams are dreams of loss. I have a young man that I have just begun to work with whose very first dream was that he was riding his bicycle on the familiar path and, suddenly, he saw a little pathway that he hadn't noticed before. That pathway went down, he said very revealingly, into a depression. Now we are walking through that depression, he and I, working at it, looking at it, seeing what's there. It is very moving. And, through that, he is definitely becoming reconnected to himself. One of the things I am having him do, because he came saying he thought maybe he was an artist, is to draw his dreams. We sit on the floor together every session and look at the drawings he has made. It is quite phenomenal.

JE: *Do you use creative methods to help people delve more deeply?*

AB: Yes, and sand tray and active imagination exercises. I will have people expand their dream a little further, like a waking dream. If a dream ends abruptly I will ask the person, "Suppose this dream went on? What do you think would happen next?" I invite them to close their eyes and recreate the dream out loud. It's a very powerful method. With kids I use sand tray almost all the time. Some kids, though, don't like the sand tray. That also is like a waking dream, putting out the symbols, taking things from the world, and I think it is always important to acknowledge the connection with the world. Putting them in the sand and then seeing what's there as a way of seeing how the self, how the soul is manifesting in the world.

JE: *Do they tell the story of what they see?*

AB: I always ask if there is anything they want to tell me about this. Frequently, children will say, "No, not really." For example, I will ask, "What's he doing over there? Or, "What's that bear doing?" Or, "What do you think is going to happen when that bear comes closer?" That kind of thing. We stay within the story.

JE: *Do you find that story telling is a method of remembering and reconnecting?*

AB: Very much. It is moving that you say that because I have been writing about just that this week. May I read it to you? [from Anita's journal]

> Certain stories I have heard in the past few weeks demand to be told. One was about a father who died and the son went to his bedside while the rabbi spoke with the others. I know he was looking at the sheet which covered his father and looked at his leg, which had been amputated, to see if God had made him whole. He was dead. The son was disappointed when He didn't.

> [And, continuing, from another journal entry]

> A friend had been riding all night in a car with a man she didn't know well. Toward dawn, they came to a field, left the car and lay in that field, watching the sky and waiting for dawn to come, seeing the waving grass, how the world reveals itself at that hour. Ever afterwards the sense of her loss was confused with that. Another child was diagnosed with a serious, large tumor on the kidney. This tumor was said to weigh six to eight pounds. The morning before the surgery, her mother piled whatever vegetables she had on the kitchen scale until she could see for herself what six to eight pounds looked like. I am not doing what I was intended to be doing, I am not writing poetry. If I am not making these stories, these moments, which otherwise would fail to be marked by anyone else, they would not be manifest. Not that there is anything particularly special about my scene, but that each of us has a particular scene. If I do not articulate

what I came here to do, regardless of whatever else I do, they will be lost. Through our stories we will be known and through our stories the world will be known. It seems so essential.

JE: *The paradox of that is when people get so wound up in the narcissistic story that the story becomes all about being seen.*

AB: Yes, people think they come to therapy to finally have somebody listen to them. I try to help them see that they are not the only ones going through these experiences. I will make connections with what they are feeling and what the earth is feeling. Or connections between what they are feeling and some sense of what is happening to women these days, or this is what is happening to single mothers these days—that kind of thing.

The other thing that I really encourage them to do is take a look at the natural world, to offer back to nature, no matter how wounded you are. I think offering back is always a way of coming back to yourself. Even with a simple thing like making a garden, or teaching a child to make a garden, I try to help them see that their individual story is part of a stream of stories that everybody has. It is a very narrow line. They do come to be heard but, on the other hand, that "totally wound up in me" is encouraged by our culture anyhow.

JE: *What tools do you give a person?*

AB: I reconnect them to a larger picture.

JE: *When do you know that something is happening? When do you see that spark?*

AB: That's a really good question. It is very subtle because sometimes there is just a feeling in the room. Sometimes there is just a little bit more energy than there was a few minutes ago. Sometimes there is a concern about something outside the self.

I saw it in a kid the other day, a little boy I have been working with. He was originally diagnosed with autism but I don't think he's an autistic child. I think he is just a child who is very tied up inside his head. He asked me spontaneously, "So what are you going to do on your holidays?" And that was a big deal, a really big deal. He was really interested and really wanted to listen.

JE: *What do you see as the role of therapy?*

AB: That's a wonderful question. I think the danger of therapy in our culture is it becomes the guardian of the middle class. I teach in a graduate psychology class and I see my students start off all their papers with: So-and-so is a such-and-such year old, ethnic man, appropriately dressed...I sort of underline that phrase. Appropriately dressed by whose standards? And that is a very good lead-in. We must not be guardians of the middle class consumer values because I think the middle class consumer values are killing us. Therapy really has to be a door into one's sense of a greater world and I see myself as a therapist being a midwife to that process. I hold the door open wider and it has to be a door into the world, not just into self, self, self. So much of the new age stuff is about self, self, self. I am this and I am that...it is boring to the point of ad nauseam.

JE: *When you are working with someone do you encourage them to write and read poetry to get a sense of their own spiritual soul, along with working with what is happening in their daily life?*

AB: I really encourage people to read and listen to things that are very nourishing. There is so much soul loss in this culture; there is so much junk. People fill their minds and their spirits with junk all the time. Very often I use poetry because poetry is always just there for me. I will recite it or I have a bookshelf in my therapy space which I call the *tirtha* (the coming together of two streams). It is a sacred place where two streams or two rivers come together. At that point where they merge is the "tirtha". I can never call it office anymore because office is out. I keep some books there and I'll pull them out and show them, saying, "What you say reminds me of a poem." I do encourage people to feed themselves on these books.

JE: *In many of the traditions that I am exploring, there seem to be themes emerging. One is story-telling as a way of remembering what has been lost. The second is the feeding and then the third is being in-spirited. I am wondering if we could talk a bit more about the feeding, in the way you work with people.*

AB: Feeding, going to the sources that give nourishment—as people through the ages have done by going to music, and the arts-what we created, we create out of our art. We need to remember. I wrote a poem, a section of a long poem, called "A Record." This section says the poem is a record of what would be lost if it were not written. Again, we have this shadow feeding in our culture, the consumer culture, where people are just gorging themselves all the time on non-nutritious stuff, from McDonald's french fries to yucky television and magazines and all that. I try to bring in references to things that will nourish. Very often I will say to a person, "You must get from the library *Moby Dick* or Bach's "Sixth Unaccompanied Cello Suite" or Mozart's "Requiem," something like that. It just feels to me that this is really important. Then there is the nourishment of silence. I talk a lot about the necessity to be still, that our culture doesn't want us to be still. Sometimes I will set assignments for people telling them just to go out for an hour and write everything down. The only reason I ask them to write it down is if you are just listening it is easy to get distracted, but if you have to write it down you pay attention. People have forgotten how to pay attention. Again, they start listening to their own silence. I do it, too. I walk the dogs five miles a day early in the morning. Sometimes I miss the walk; sometimes I am so tied up in my own head that I miss the walk. I come home and say that I've just moved my legs five miles and where was I? I work when I see that happening in myself. This morning I was out about a quarter past five; it was gorgeous and I was just marveling at all the different birds, their songs, their little flights from tree to tree...it was wonderful. That's feeding.

JE: *There doesn't seem to be a spiritual foundation in our culture.*

AB: There isn't a spiritual underpinning. People don't seek it; it is not encouraged in our culture. I have always had it and I think it is what saved me. I was brought up in a very dysfunctional, abusive family, a really unbelievably dysfunctional family. It is amazing that all my mother's children didn't die. One of the children did die, but it is incredible that any of us survived. .

I don't know where I got this from. My grandfathers, both rabbis, were dead by the time I was six. And I didn't know my mother's father all that well; he only spoke Yiddish so I couldn't really communicate with him, although I could some. My father's father was a very sweet, sort of melancholy man. I think it was right after he died that I started writing poetry - I was six. There was some thread there that followed, and I attribute whatever I have to the spiritual seeking which resulted.

JE: *How do you feel we can engender that in our world?*

AB: It is a really important question and I deal with it all the time, especially having raised two children. What I did with my own children...when I look at it now, we didn't do much! Other people do projects - we didn't do projects. I think we used to go to the beach or the park and just look at the trees, the light, the shadows...a lot of that, just noting and being aware and being present. I do that with my little granddaughter too. She doesn't have language yet but that doesn't seem to matter. I think singing is also important, anything that invokes spirit. I wanted more rituals, that was one thing I wanted. I wanted us to sing before dinner; I wanted us to have something we could do together and, because I wanted it, they didn't want it! But now I see Nora bringing up her daughter and she wants to do that kind of thing today. I think that kind of thing is good and also we need to simply things, keep things from getting too rushed and too competitive. I look at the kids and they are all so worried about what college they can get into. I think it is part of the "industrial growth society" as Joanna Macy called it. We get so caught up in it.

JE: *It is what Alice Miller calls "soul murder." Where is there an opportunity to be a child?*

AB: I'll give another example. Sue is a nervous wreck. She is a sophomore in high school. Every breath she takes is to get into college. It is so cruel to see. She can't eat, she can't sleep, she can't enjoy her friends. She is always depressed, she cries all the time, and she works hours and hours and hours a day. She's not here. And with all the things she is doing, she's not working hard enough.

JE: *How are you working with her? .*

AB: I try to help her reach down into where she is now. We found two things. She really loves to swim (and she is actually going to spend this summer teaching swimming to kids); she loves moving her body. If she can just get into her body and be in the water and the warm air, it is going to be good for her. The second thing she loves is poetry. We talk a lot about poetry. I also tell her a lot about my own self. I really remember well what it was like to be that age and so confused and so driven. I felt this burden on my shoulders. I was already writing poetry, the best poet that ever lived, I thought.

JE: *Do you see your life as a series of remembering?*

AB: It is very visceral and I think that is what my poetry is about. I think my poetry is making an articulation of this. There is one poem I wrote about....I was pregnant with a baby who died half way through the pregnancy; I was five months pregnant with her...I was very, very sad for the loss afterwards. I was standing by the kitchen window and we had a cat, whose name was Lucia, and I watched her one morning when I was filled with this sorrow; it was foggy and it was summer and I watched her walk across the garden, and my life came back. It really was that - it was just something like watching her walk across the garden in the fog and my life came back.

JE: *How does the soul return? When does it happen? It is available to us but we keep missing ourselves.*

AB: Exactly. It happens a lot, for me anyway, it happens through that kind of thing - just a sudden moment. I was describing it to my friend, who is really the deep friend of my soul more than anybody has been in this lifetime. At that moment she spoke and was telling me this story as we were taking a walk together. She is sixty now. It was forty years ago when she told me that story, and I could feel the effect that moment had had on her life. Those moments are huge. Awakening of the soul and revealing the woe, I think they are very common together. It is something about opening our eyes and perceiving it was there all the time. Anything we are looking at now could be that, if we had that leaning. The world and us, the world and us, and there is no separation. I think those moments also come in the presence of two people being together, how we can mutually inspire and infuse each other's spirits.

JE: *How can we raise our awareness for our culture and our society to remember?*

AB: I think that those of us who are thinking about these things need to do it by example, by speaking about it, by using models. People respond. You know we are into such big things now...our culture, our president, this whole mess. It gets worse and worse. I don't even open the newspaper. For three months I didn't even get the paper and then all of a sudden I started getting it and another one started coming. It was like they multiplied, and I didn't subscribe. They wanted me to have it, whoever "they" were. It is such a mess on the collective scale but I think we can't give up. You are not obligated to complete the work but neither are you free to desist from it. Maybe we are not going to get there but we can't not try to get there.

    I've been doing a lot of music in the last couple of years, a lot of singing, a lot of instrument playing. Joanna Macy became kind of intrigued about the music I was playing and said, "Why don't you come to some of my workshops and we'll sing a lament?" So I wrote a lament. The first one we did was in Monterey on the weekend that Bush was inaugurated. We had about two hundred people in the group, and we sang for over an hour. I just gave them the form of this lament, and they made up the verses. It was really, really helpful. We did it twice more together—once in spirit walk and once in the Buddhist priory. It was really powerful just getting people to grieve together.

I think we need more collective forms of grief. I think we need to start with that. We have had this image that we should go and rent the Coliseum or Yankee Stadium. Go grieve. People are feeling horrible, people are feeling defeated, and we need to get it out and into the world. We need to be able to say to each other "Shit! This is what's happening to all the world!" I do think this is a collective form that we could work with.

I am trying very hard to finish a play on which I got sort of stuck, for ego reasons. I didn't think it was good enough. But I think I want to finish it because it is a play about Rosa Luxemburg's life. She was a great revolutionary and the one who was never heard of for herself, even though she was in prison for four years. I will read you a quote that I have up here. I will read it in German and then translate it for you. She says, "A world has to be loved but every tear that flows, even though it may be wiped away, is an accusation. A person who is hurrying on to do great, important things and, in his hurrying, he crushes a worm with brutal inattention." I love that, really love that. So I think I have to finish that play and give it away so that it can be performed. I think we need forms of art and ritual that help awaken people. I think those of us who have the capacity to do that are obligated now to do it. It is an obligation, a holy service.

JE: *When you visit Croatia soon, how will you work with the children?*

AB: I am bringing some sand tray toys for use. I am going to be doing some music. I am going to be doing some of the work that I have learned doing workshops with Joanna Macy on despair, helping the kids articulate what they are feeling in whatever ways they can, and then define some way of coming together. Also, a lot of simple stuff, I think, just holding them and listening to them and taking them for walks, looking at things together, and swimming—just very simple things of being together.

JE: *Did you do that when you went to India and worked with children?*

AB: Yes, that was two winters ago when I went for a month. We did the same kind of things, being together. More and more I find I want to do that. I want to go out in the world and work with groups. I like to work one-on-one but I also want to work with groups.

JE: *There is so much stimulus happening around us. We have failed to rest, integrate, and rejuvenate.*

AB: Also in the spiritual context, absolutely. Quests for the questing. We are moving from one thing to another, one experience after another. A friend of mine wrote a beautiful piece on what she called "reverberation." We don't allow ourselves reverberation. We go from one thing to the next. We don't give ourselves time to digest what we just did, and it is dangerous.

So there is that paradox between being "out" in the world, doing your spirit/heart work, and being "in" the world and doing the heart work, balancing. It is sort of the point on the exclamation mark of everything.

JE: *How do we come back into balance?*

AB: We have to come back into balance and see what is really important, see what part we can hold, what part the people can hold, trust that other people will hold the concepts.

JE: *Do you have trust?*

AB: I do. I don't know why because certainly everything in my childhood would argue against it. I will tell you a story. When I was two-and-a-half years old my mother and I were walking by the water, along the Atlantic ocean, and I was in the waves, the undertow had pulled me into the water. My mother let go of me. My mother swam a mile every day in that ocean, but she just stood there. I was drowning, and I have had memories of that drowning come back to me in a lot of body work sessions when I can feel suffocation, my arms feeling very tired. Somebody came to save me, somebody who didn't know me, somebody I never saw again in my life. Some man came and pulled me out. I was very traumatized. I didn't talk for the next three days. But somebody came.

My mother would tell the story as if it were her story. "I was just devastated; my child was drowning." But I think I learned that I could trust the world, that somebody would be there, somebody's arms would hold me and pull me out. It happened over and over again in my childhood. I was always being taken in by people, invited to other people's families. On a personal level, I learned to trust that there was goodness in the world and that there was awareness in the world.

My friends say to me that I am so bold, so fearless. I don't think that's a big deal. Really bad things happen and I survive. I have some faith that we can get through. I don't necessarily trust that we can save the world. I think we are in deep trouble. I worry about that with my granddaughter, just for all those beautiful things out there. But I do have a basic concept of the good intentions of many people, not everybody, but many, many people who can be awakened and be moved. I think I couldn't get out of bed if I didn't have that.

I also have trust in some process that we don't really know about. We don't know what it is that is bringing us to this or that, why should that happen in our lives, but there is no point in not trusting and resisting it because there is a lot of energy wasted. It's going to happen anyhow. So I have learned to trust. I don't worry very much now. I don't like it when something feels threatening.

There is a path that has to be followed. I don't know what it is but I yield to it. I trust in the wisdom and process. I don't know why I am able to do that but I am very grateful because I think it has brought me riches. Why I am able to make that choice is a mystery but it is there. I think that somewhere I trust that I am helping, and therein lies the health of my soul.

June 20, 2001

Oakland, California

JE: *Continuing with the Doctoral degree of Creation Spirituality-in-the-world theme from your address to the graduating Doctor of Ministry students, as the elder of this school, I want to ask you about the epidemic of soul loss. What do you see as the main contributing factors? How do you feel about where we are now and where we are going?*

MF: The language of "soul loss" has something very poetic about it, something spiritual and big--because it's a big thing that is draining away from us. It suggests that everything from our values to our communities to all our relationships are distorted. One example of this distortion is the infinite number of distractions (i.e., addictions) that our culture offers us on a daily basis. Instead of soul food, we are being offered junk--ersatz, pseudo soul food. This food fails to nourish the deepness of the soul. Instead, it taps into desire, it taps into little things that the soul wants without going into the soul's longing and to the deepness of the soul. It's what the mystics have always said—it's about the outer instead of the inner. It's about the superficial instead of the deep. And it goes on and on. Our economy of consumerism is built on turning us into consumers and consumers of trivia. The soul doesn't live on trivia. So much of the media—including television, news, political speeches, advertising—is trivia.

One of my favorite books is *The Age of Missing Information* by Bill McGibbon (such a funny book but scary too). The book covers a period of 24 hours in America in which chapters alternate between what is going on in television, and what is going on in a pond. In this one-day period, I don't remember the date exactly, the author went to a pond for 24 hours. He found 150 friends who taped 150 channels on television so he had a record of what was going on on television for a 24- hour period, while he lived out what was going on at the pond in nature. So it is just amazing to go from one world to the other—on the one hand "I Love Lucy" and all these crazy game shows which most people are at home watching versus what the ducks are teaching you and what jumping into a cold pond is teaching you. It's a brilliant work; both funny and a scathing indictment of culture at the same time. It's exactly what you are talking about: soul loss--it's being sucked into the television set.

Another example of soul loss is, of course, abuse. I met a group of friends from Latin America. They told their stories about escaping from Latin America, fleeing here, and the abuse of all kinds that they had endured; and, in the process, how their souls had been stolen. There was so much grief there; there was so much pain. The beautiful thing is that they are still alive in many ways; they can still laugh; they have a value system. I'm sure you come across in your work too how amazingly strong the human can be to endure what we endure.

I think men are more lost than women in our culture. "Father Sky" has been shut down to us for centuries. We were told sky is inert and dead--nothing but a machine. We were also told that about the Earth but no one really believed it because the flowers came up every spring and the vegetables come up and things are living; so therefore it is harder to believe that nonsense about "Mother Earth" being inert. The Sky, well, we kind of shrug our shoulders and say, "That's it—a dead place." What does that do to Fatherhood? What does this do to the male soul wanting to grow? Of course this teaching served a political purpose by shrinking our soul so that we fit into the industrial factory context of work. Life is nothing but bringing a paycheck home to the kids and watching television and kind of living a fantasy life of "if I had been a football player" or "if I could buy this kind of car."

But with the new cosmology the sky is not dead. Rather it is very beautiful, creative, amazing and full of life and death and divine wisdom. So the shift is possible. I think the loss of cosmology, the shut down of the cosmos, has a lot to do with the draining of the soul. I think men in a way pay more of a price because I think women are closer to the Earth. I think they have found ways to live alternative lives. They haven't taken in depression ideology of our patriarchal institutions so theirs is not as toxic as the male soul. It's still there in all of us. I think of my mother whom we just buried a week ago. She didn't buy into everything the politicians said. She never gave her soul away. I think many men give their souls away at work and, in a way, there is kind of no place else to give it. I think it is a special male problem.

There was a doctor in class who told a powerful story about a very bright guy, very interested in science and not interested in religion. He thought that science had the answers, and he was very much a materialist—very interested in consuming and making a lot of money. But then he had an alcohol problem and in AA he woke up to this other side of psyche, the spiritual side, and it just shifted his whole ground of being. To think how many other men have to go through that to find out they have a soul. There are a lot of people, a lot of men especially, who have bought the modern view of the world which is soul-less. This generates a race for things and it is a competitive race.

JE: *What do you feel would assist men in waking up?.*

MF: Maturity and cosmology; and, of course, spiritual practice, ceremonies, ritual, a sense of community. Robert Bly says men learn only in ritual. I think it's an amazing statement even if it's only 50% right. If men only learn what's important in ritual, then where are the rituals where men are learning? That is where it gets really scary because our rituals are so tepid and really without power in the white world today. That's why our Techno-Cosmic Mass is very important and very powerful. Because, while still tapping into our historical church traditions, they elicit power through dance. Hence the artists who are drawn to it to really make something happen. Obviously the recovery and sharing of traditions and indigenous rituals is redemptive. For me personally, I wouldn't have survived without Native American ceremonies of Sundance, Sweat Lodge, and prayer. My spirituality for 20-25 years has been supported by Native American ritual. This is the gift of the pre-modern people.

JE: *Do you feel that through the ceremonies that you recovered parts of yourself that have been fragmented?*

MF: I wouldn't put it that way about myself. What I would say is I deepened what I was given in my tradition, and I was able to hold onto what was most important in my tradition. And to get strong so I could stand up to those forces that wanted to silence me or tell me that I was on the wrong path or that what I felt was not important. So it made me strong. But it also took me to a place of unity, of community and of listening and depth that I needed, but that I didn't find in most Christian forms of worship at that time. In my training years ago, we did a lot of meditation work and a lot of soul deepening came my way. However, I did notice from conversations with many other Dominicans that a lot of them were not so affected by the practices as I had been. I had never felt that my soul was all that fragmented. In my autobiography, *Confessions of a Post-Denominational Priest*, I recall an incident in my life when I was twelve or thirteen, that set me on a different path. I lost my legs to polio, and that event set me on another course. While I was in the hospital, I met a Dominican brother who was very different from my father, very contemplative; he ended up being a Trappist monk. He introduced me, just by his joy, to the contemplative and mystical dimension of being a man and that gave me another definition of being a man. I got my legs back. That surprised the doctors and it didn't fit the formula, but the entire experience gave me a different perspective. So having polio was in a way a rite of passage for me.

Also, I was facing death because I had a friend who had died a year before from polio. This strengthened me and was a unique rite of passage. At the age of twenty, entering the Dominicans, entering a brotherhood was another deep rite of passage—this, too, was very rare in my generation. In retrospect, the three vows of *poverty, celibacy,* and *obedience* were a challenge, an adventure, and all the things a rite of passage needs to be.

JE: *Do you feel shame is a motivator or a contributor to soul loss, particularly in men in our culture?*

MF: My father was a conservative Catholic; he went to an Augustine Catholic School. For a lot of Catholics, there is guilt. There is obviously a difference between guilt and shame. Shame, speaking from a Catholic background, has been taught to us around our having a sexual body. In Augustine and St. Paul too, we have been taught to be ashamed of our sexuality. This shame has served political purposes. It confused people terribly.

Seneca woman José Hobday said, "There are no Indians who believe in the original sin. We had to memorize the words when it was time for catechism in order to tell the priest what he wanted to hear." Many women have told me of the experience, painful but mystical, in giving birth; and you know you wouldn't do that if you're just bringing sin into the world. Through Saint Augustine, birth and the body and sexuality were sources of shame. Birth got linked to original sin. So I think that shame is a shadow side of Christianity. We still see it in the church and in the hierarchical teachings. Why did they overreact to my book *Original Blessings* except that they are invested in original sin? They so overreacted that they were misquoting; they didn't read it right. To think you can run religion without shame, you know, I think that's what they really don't believe.

JE: *It's obvious.*

MF: Yes it's obvious in our culture. I maintain that the whole advertising industry is built on a fall/redemption ideology of shame. Look at any ad and it's about how you need to be saved by some outside intervention (a secular version of Full-Redemption religion), such as toothpaste or a refrigerator, and it's appealing to shame. We are told that we don't measure up in some way. But we can buy our way out; and, of course, this goes back to what we talked about earlier—the superficiality, the external. If you are looking at just the external, we are set up to not care.

JE: *One of the things I look at in advertising is how the "Great Mother" Earth is used – they park a Jeep on top of a sacred place and, if you have this Jeep, you will have this sacred experience.*

MF: The arrogance of it all; de-sacralizing sacred land—to sell an automobile! The first time I heard Beethoven's Ninth Symphony used as an advertisement, I was deeply offended. They will take anything. I've even seen, I think, some of my work in these advertisements—they are starting to use words like "Awe," and "Wonder" and "Sacred." Those words have become the new buzz words. Once I met someone in an audience when I was speaking who was there to get new words that were fresh. Advertisers steal our language—find out some fresh words and take them home and hijack them, incorporating them into advertising. It's really scary. Hijackers of sacred beings and sacred words.

JE: *How do we go about remembering our true potential?*

MF: Ritual is always an act of remembering. Rabbi Heschel says, "All of Jewish worship can be summarized in one word and that is: "Remember." Creativity is the key. That is why art as meditation is so powerful—it is about paying attention to our memories. We need to go inward to find our images. I remember a student some years ago who was forty-one and he took massage as meditation; in that course he remembered that he had been sexually abused by an aunt every Friday afternoon for a year when he was seven years old. But from the age of seven to forty-one, he had forgotten that. Imagine how much energy it took to shut down his memory for thirty-four years. Because of art as meditation, he was liberated and freed by remembering. There are so many kinds of meditation. Meditation is about getting at the child in ourselves. And, of course, this man's body itself also carried the memory. It follows that bodywork is a necessary way to remember. If we split body from soul, we don't remember our totality. We are lost. Lost souls, lost bodies. They do go together after all.

JE: *What part does hope and despair play in our culture?*

MF: Despair can be a bridge to hope, because then truth can begin to come out. Also, I believe in humanity's creativity; just as some people are doing great damage with our creativity, nevertheless we also do great good. For example, we really could totally reinvent the way we are getting energy. I watched a videotaped interview with grounded people—generals, astronauts, engineers--who came out at a press conference about UFO's. They said these UFO's are powered through gravity, a totally renewable source of energy. They are machines that can go 10,000 miles an hour powered entirely by gravity. This discovery could totally reinvent energy for our entire species. The reason that this has been covered up is that the oil corporations persuaded the government to squelch the truth. It really does not make sense.

Vehicles are being manufactured now that average 120 miles per gallon. The fact is creativity gives possibilities and possibilities give hope.

I heard Buckminster Fuller speak a number of years ago. He was an engineer, a man with vision and compassion. He said, "With the knowledge we had then (that was probably fifteen to twenty years ago), we could feed everybody in the world, clothe everybody in the world, provide healthcare for everybody in the world, educate everybody in the world in two-and-a-half years." "But," he said, "we have to have the will to set aside other priorities for awhile to get it done." I've often thought if we had taken that two-and-a-half years to accomplish these things fifteen to twenty years ago, where would we be now as a species?

Consider the building of the Bay Bridge. We drive over the Bay Bridge and it seems like a highway, but it isn't a highway— it's a miracle! When constructed in the 1930's, it was the biggest suspension bridge ever built by human beings. They had to face all kinds of problems. The genius of it was they really built three bridges—one bridge to the concrete slab in the middle (which is deeper than the Empire State Building), one bridge from the concrete to the island, then one bridge from the island to the shore. And it works. I drive on it regularly; it had better work! The story about how many lives were lost, how many intellectual battles were fought, and problems were solved in its making is awesome. Also, look at what we do when we go to war. Why can't we expend that enormous creative energy towards a position of survival? That gives me hope. Get the word out about how truly dire things are. There were protests against Bush and U.S. policies during the recent Kyoto talks and in the political theatres in Europe. Europeans are not in as much denial as Americans. No one could be in as much denial as Americans. The American agenda is to be an Empire.

JE: *Are we in a depressed culture, are we operating out of despair?*

MF: "Despair," an interesting choice of language. Aquinas says despair is not the worst, but it is the most dangerous of all sins, why? Because, when you are in despair, you are indifferent to what you do to yourself and others. And it leads to addictions, to self-abuse, and to violence. And so, when you mention depression, that is serious. Cosmology teaches that people have to learn we are not here by chance; we had a fifteen billion year ride getting here.

There is hope in the universe. You are not going to get hope from a government, or get it from our churches unfortunately; but the universe has never let us down.

JE: *Do you feel the collective consciousness of humanity is ripe for spiritual takeover?*

MF: We are desperate for the next step in spirituality. We cannot expect government or institutions or religion or family alone to bring about the transformation. The biggest, deepest changes coming through are spiritual. I feel the return to the Christian tradition and the work that has been done on the historical Jesus has been very very valuable. It allowed us to understand more of the history of Jesus and what he brought us, not just what the church has said. We have opened to the Cosmic Christ and teachings which are really universal in relation to other teachings. Everything is sacred; everything is not based on hierarchy. I think once we see that and experience it, spirituality becomes really very simple. It must be. We have to travel very lightly in the next millennium in terms of our spiritual baggage. Healthy monks like Thich Nhat Hahn, His Holiness the Fourteenth Dalai Lama, Bede Griffiths and others are taking the concentrated lessons learned in monastic practice and making them accessible for everyone. Bede Griffiths told me before he died to "pitch" monasticism to the lay people. The end of the age of Pisces is the end of dualism—the separation of monk and lay person. Now, in the present age, all of us have to learn meditation forms to calm the reptilian brain.

JE: *Any other comments?*

MF: Do not underestimate the powers of the Mother, the powers of recovering the feminine. The Goddess has been so neglected in mainline western consciousness for so long. When the Goddess is recovered, don't underestimate the power to reinvent things. We are not here alone; we have angels and ancestors helping us. The Universe has invested a lot in us. We are very close to messing it up. Here's a concrete example of that that makes me laugh. Years ago a woman who was suffering from depression told me she had tried therapy for many years with no relief. One day a dream told her to go to the bookstore. As she was walking along looking at books at eye level, this book came down from above, hit her on the head, and fell on the floor. It was my book on Meister Eckhart. She had never heard of him or me, but that book hit her on the head. She took the book home, read it, and it totally cured her. What that says to me is that there are angels in bookstores! They may not be in churches anymore, but they are in bookstores and they're busy.

I do think recovering mystical experiences in all aspects of practices and revelations is a gift—it gives people hope. Hope teaches us about the mystic in us. There is a lot of room for that to grow in our culture.

University of Creation Spirituality D.Min.
Graduation Day Speech

June 17, 2001

Matthew Fox

It is a great joy and a fulfillment of a dream to stand before you and announce the largest class ever to graduate from UCS with a doctoral degree in creation spirituality. I praise all forty-three graduates for your dedication and hard work; I praise the faculty for theirs and the staff and administration of the University—its board and its supporters.

Here at UCS we are trying to develop work, deepen it, deconstruct and reconstruct work. Here we are trying to fill in the gaps in our professional training and education—all of us, no matter what profession we come from. Years ago when I was speaking to the Episcopal bishop about the need for the Techno Cosmic Mass I said: "I believe that boredom at worship is ecumenical. All denominations are suffering from it." So here, in the context of reinventing work, I believe it can be said that ALL of our professions have been stripped of their sacred dimensions and are equally out of touch with their spiritual dimension. Business, education, psychology, art, engineering, medicine, religion too—all of them have missed in great part the spiritual dimension of their vocations.

Our professional schools and degree granting institutions rarely if ever trained us in the new cosmology that teaches us reverence for existence: of the "Is-ness of God." They did not teach us our sacred relationship with all things—the stars, the universe, the animals, the sky, the waters, the forests and including our own bodies, minds and imaginations. And they rarely if ever taught us spiritual practices that engage the lower as well as upper charkas. This sin of omission sets us up for devaluating the earth, for being disconnected and cut off from the earth and her powers and our power of imagination as co-creators.

Here at UCS we consciously and deliberately do what Bell Hooks says we must do: "set in motion an aesthetic revolution." For here we honor the cosmology and the creativity that our species discovers and gives birth to. We also honor what Wes Jackson calls "our species' strongest suit"—our ignorance. We should lead with our strongest suit he says, which is our ignorance. For we are very conscious that the *forms* in which European models of education operate are ignorant and carry-on ignorance--ignoring our deepest self, ignoring our powers of imagination, ignoring earth, ignoring space/time and cosmology. Ignorance—and ignoring—the lower chakras including the middle heart charka. Ignorance of compassion and eco-justice, of our powers of creativity and our relationship to the whole (cosmos). Art as meditation, body prayer, ritual, the mystics and New Cosmology are our medicines at UCS against this ignorance and ignoring.

You might say that here at UCS we are challenging the 3 R's of education with the 3 C's: Cosmology (including context and community); Creativity and Compassion. Without these, the 3 C's, we have no context, no meaning, no substance, no spirit.

What makes work deep? When it draws on these 3 C's and contributes to them: (1) Cosmology—our work in the context of history of the universe, of space and time; (2) Creativity—our work as creative work, as giving birth to problem-solving, to new connection-making, to joy itself. (3) Compassion—how our work passes on both celebration and justice. You cannot have one without the other.

There are three myths that are behind this degree and the University of Creation Spirituality. Why does it matter, namely, that we pass on new myths in our time? Rollo May says: "Myth is the foundation of values and ethics." Remember that a myth is not an untruth. It is a truth too big for a mere factoid, too big for a mere bumper sticker. The three myths governing this school are as follows.

- By changing work we can change history. The key to transformation *is* the transformation of work.
- Cosmology matters. It gives us the *context* by which to understand our place in time and space. Therefore we must bring the word "universe" back to university and, hopefully, challenge other educational institutions to do the same. It gives us the sense of community that anthropocentrism has killed. It heals cosmic loneliness.
- Creativity matters. Creativity is the only thing our species really has going for it. Why aren't we making creativity the centerpiece of educational renewal? Why aren't we learning to discipline our imaginations and creativity and bring them into the ethical projects that so challenge our species today? It is because our creativity, like everything else in our culture,

has been desacralized, cut off from our spiritual traditions and therefore part of the problem and not part of the solution. Art as meditation heals this split between creativity and spirit. It encourages us to recover our sense of co-creation with the Divine Creative Spirit that both "hovered over the waters at the beginning of creation and hovers over the mind of the artist at work" (Aquinas).

In treating Deep Ecumenism in my book, *One River, Many Wells,* I lay out eighteen themes that all our religions and spiritual traditions can agree on as vital themes for our survival--themes like creation, light, suffering, compassion, holy imagination, etc. I treated work as a theme in my book, *The Reinvention of Work* where I draw on the major spiritual traditions of the world to listen to what they say and agree on regarding the reinvention of work. For example, that joy and work go together. "In work, do what you enjoy" (Tao te Ching). "They all attain perfection when they find joy in their work" (Bhagavad Gita).

The way our program has developed here at UCS is so gratifying to me at still another level and that is the deep ecumenism of our professions themselves and the deep ecumenism that must go on within our professions. About the former, I mean the experience you have had of rubbing shoulders, business people with clergy, artists with engineers, social workers with educators, therapists with doctors. Here we are working from a common ground—that of the spirituality of our work; and, therefore, we have much in common. And you educate one another; you don't have everything in common.

Diversity is alive as well. Yet by meeting both intellectually in your seminars and creatively in art as medication and body prayer, you find your deeper sense of common ground--the place where we all work from a common source and therefore find some common "enchantment" in our work (to use Meister Eckhart's language). "Grace escapes the soul so that it now no longer accomplishes things with grace but divinely in God. Thus the soul is in a wonderful way enchanted and loses itself." Our work "draws all its being from nowhere else but from and in the heart of God."

Regarding deep ecumenism within our professions themselves, I point to a man I met a few years ago in upstate New York who was a medical doctor. But he was devoting his life to what he called "medical ecumenism," i.e. bringing together the different traditions of healing: M.D.'s, acupuncturists, chiropractors, herbalists, etc. He was very wise. We need to bring together within our professions themselves a deep ecumenism.

I have an image that came to me this week about work and professions that I want to leave with this graduating class. You know about the charkas, these seven energy points in our physical and emotional and spiritual bodies. The word charka in Sanskrit you will recall means "intersection." I invite you to think of our professions themselves as chakras of the body politic, chakras of the mystical body of Christ or the Buddha Body, the Cosmic Body, the Body of the Cosmic Christ. For that is what they are. Our professions are power points, intersections where ideas, traditions, actions, all come together. They need detoxing; they need cleaning up. They need to return to their spiritual source and their spiritual center. They are intersections where our spiritual powers and professional power come together around love. They are about love—how we bless one another in community. This indeed constitutes the reinvention of work.

As you graduates go into your profession again with this special degree, a Doctorate in Creation Spirituality, remember the words of Meister Eckhart: "A person works in a stable. A person has breakthrough. What do they do? They return to the stable." As you return to your stables, remember us here at UCS; we are with you. We are even watching you. We expect great things from you in reinventing your work and profession. You are agents of transformation, you are spiritual warriors, you are prophets called to interfere in the abusive misuse of power in our professions and to steer that power to something worthy of our species: to a context of being part of a whole community and Cosmology; to creativity; to compassion. Remember what Hafiz teaches about the spiritual warrior: "You could become a victorious horseperson and carry your heart through this world like a life-giving sun only if you and God become sweet Lovers!" We expect nothing less. Remember us by sending able students our way; and even some financial support as well. Remember that you are leaving here with stoles as well as diplomas—that signifies that you are ministers, you are priests, you are midwives of grace *precisely* insofar as you are putting creation spirituality into practice and principles into your work worlds. And remember the words of Hildegard of Bingen. "Be not lax in celebrating…Be ablaze with enthusiasm. Let us be an alive, burning offering before the altar of God!"

May your work be deep, may it draw on the wisdom of the mystic-prophets, the spiritual warriors who have gone before you in your own professions. May it reach the depths of others' hearts and lives. May we eschew all shallowness, pettiness and externalities for that inwardness and innerness that is the meaning, the deep meaning of spirit. As Eckhart put it: "Your outward work can never be small if the inward one is great; and the outward work can never be great or good if the inward is small or of little worth. The inward work always includes in itself all size, all breadth and all length."

May you have the magnanimity, the greatness of soul and bigness of spirit and courage to re-sacralize our culture by bringing the sacred back to education, to work, to your citizenship and to all your relations. If you do that, you will all graduate summa cum laude, with the highest praise. That will happen not today; but when you breathe your last breath and return your spirit to the greater breath of the universe. Until then, work hard, play hard, laugh often and disturb the pseudo peace!

INTERVIEW WITH
SANDRA INGERMAN

September 19, 2001

Santa Fe, New Mexico

JE: *I am interested in the source of your soul retrieval training. Did the spirits give you this form that you are teaching? How did you arrive at it?*

SI: I heard Michael Harner say the words "soul retrieval" at a workshop in the early eighties, but he didn't teach anything about it. I was assisting him in a workshop around 1985 when a woman came up to me and asked me for some healing help. She had a disturbing journey about her father who had crossed over. During her journey she saw she needed to forgive him for the sexual abuse from her childhood. I thought that I was going to do a shamanic extraction for her. What sounded logical to me was to extract the pain that was in her heart. I agreed to meet with her before the workshop started. I was staying at a friend's house where she drove out to meet me. I did a diagnostic journey for the extraction of taking out the pain in her heart. My power animal said that was not what she needed. He took me to the piece of herself that she had lost during her sexual abuse and said, "What she is dealing with is soul loss and I am going to show you how to do a soul retrieval." For bringing the soul part back, he showed me the same method used for power animal retrievals. It's the same system. The actual mechanics of power animal retrievals I had learned from Michael Harner. The theory around soul loss and how to work with retrieving souls - that there are split off parts of ourselves, fragments, all of that – I learned from the spirits.

JE: *So you began to do the soul retrievals and it has really developed and grown since then?*

SI: Yes, I have learned a lot about language. My biggest challenge has been to bridge ancient spiritual methods into a modern day, psychologically sophisticated culture. It was a challenge beyond anything I had imagined. I learned about the power of telling healing stories and how the stories that you hear in indigenous cultures are not the healing stories for people in this culture. The example I use a lot is, if you go to Siberia or to different shamans in South America, the classic story that you will hear is where the community shows up to support the soul retrieval and the shaman talks about how he or she had to battle evil spirits for the soul. When the soul is returned, the shaman talks about the victory. Everybody celebrates the victory. The client is expecting to hear that there was going to be a battle and a victory, the community is expecting to hear that there was going to be a battle and a victory. That's a healing story in these cultures. If you tell a person in the United States today that you had to battle evil spirits to get their soul and that you were victorious, they cannot (and we have tons of evidence) hear the victory. They get lost in the fact that there was a battle with evil for their souls. Shamans were, and are, the psychologists of their community. They knew the words that their clients and communities needed to hear in order to heal. It goes back to the power of imagination and telling the stories that would stimulate people's imaginations to heal.

What I have learned, in training people to do soul retrievals and in working with my own clients, is how to tell healing stories that inspire people today. Today we need stories that don't plant seeds of fear. People don't need any more fear; they need inspiration. Also, we need people to get out of the psychological jargon of inner child work when working with shamanic healing. I had to work with starting to talk about bringing back your essence, instead of pieces of the soul. When you start talking about bringing back parts of the soul in this culture people start to give those parts a personality. For example, I might be told, "My five-year-old is scared." Wait a second, I thought you got back your essence. I have been using the word "essence" instead of "soul" with people today. The intention of the journey I tell clients I will be using beforehand, and the intention I train practitioners to use is, "I am looking for any lost soul parts that are willing to come back to help that person at this point in time." The two key words are "willing" and "help" so that people can't come back with "my five-year-old doesn't want to be here". We must get out of the psychological traps so we can do our spiritual work successfully.

JE: *Is that staying in the infant stage where the very young stay without being self responsible? Is it recycling back into story without soul growth?*

SI: Right. I train people I'm working with in the language of explaining soul retrievals. For example, "I brought back pure essence that left because you were scared when you were seven." I didn't bring you back a scared seven-year-old. I am being really clear about this distinction.

There is a tremendous amount of work with vocabulary that needs to be explored. I stress this constantly during my five-day soul retrieval trainings. People are susceptible and they pick up on words, they take them in just like you plant a seed in the earth. I think that's been where I have had to shift the work and be absolutely strong... to get practitioners to understand the power of words, the power of language, and that there is a way to by-pass the psychological trap that people in this culture will try to recycle back into.

JE: *When someone takes a workshop do they leave calling themselves shamans?*

SI: I try to get them not to. I lecture about it over and over. I also talk about how I have been disappointed about the level of humility that I see in spiritual teachers and in people practicing shamanism. We can't take credit for the work, that is not what shamanism is about. It's about the spirits doing the work and it's bad luck to call yourself a shaman. There are certain ethical principles that I tend to repeat at workshops. I would hope that people coming out of my workshops are not calling themselves shamans. I really make fun of people putting "Shaman" on their business card. What I have seen is that if you do one good soul retrieval, word of mouth spreads it like wildfire. Word of mouth is how shamans get clients. One's community calls you a shaman; you don't claim this for yourself. When I see a lot of advertising going on I question the skills of the practitioner.

JE: *What do you feel has been happening in our nation as a result of the September 11th terrorist attack, from the point of view of soul loss?*

SI: It is important to remember, from a shamanic point of view, that soul loss is a survival mechanism. It comes with any kind of shock. Whether the pain is emotional or physical, it's how we avoid the full impact of the pain. Some people tell me they took a workshop on soul retrieval and they learned how to avoid soul loss. That viewpoint confuses me because soul loss is really how we survive pain. Some of us go away so that we can survive emotional and physical pain that is occurring to us at the time. I can't figure out why somebody would want to avoid soul loss. I would hope that my soul would leave if I was falling eighty floors out of a building. I think the shock is starting to wear off for us as a people from the events of September 11th. There is personal soul loss and a tremendous amount of fear.

We have always been dealing with soul loss in this country. I do not blame this country for the terrorist attacks. What I say, in my soul retrieval workshops, is people who put money over life, which is what has been happening in this country, who are willing to pollute the environment, throw chemicals in the river for the purpose of financial gain, this behavior is symptomatic of soul loss. Any time material objects are favored over life, we are looking at soul loss.

Another symptom of soul loss is addictions. We look to outside things to fill up those empty spaces inside of ourselves…whether it is drugs or alcohol, food, work, relationships or more cars, etc. We have been a country completely in a state of soul loss. In our culture we don't have spiritual foundations any more. We do have organized religion but, on the whole, we don't have spiritual practices. There is an emptiness in people, trying to fill up those empty spaces and reaching out for external kinds of things. The thinking is one more car, one more house, one more VCR and I will feel whole. We have been experiencing soul loss as a country at the time of the terrorist attack. There is emotional shock which is causing more soul loss for people. You can really see in the news how people are dealing with it through a reaction of fear, a reaction of anger, and desire for restrictions. The government is into restrictions right now on how we can make our country safe.

In my recent web page article I talked about how there is no safe place out there as long as we are in a body. Bodies aren't safe. Spiritually, we are always safe because the spirit never dies. It will be interesting to watch, as a culture, how people are willing to compromise freedom for an illusion of safety. I see there is a lot of outer reaction from fear and anger, instead of going inside of ourselves and trying to find peace and in trying to find different kinds of solutions. Soul loss is indicated whenever we keep looking to our external world.

JE: *Do you see this as being a really defining moment in our spiritual evolution?*

SI: Yes, I definitely do. I could actually feel things building up to this. Something had to shift. Everybody knew there was a shift coming. I know I definitely felt that something very big was coming. I think the shift and change could go any way because there is such a shadow side to spiritual work, too. I was actually teaching a workshop on soul retrieval training when this happened. There were forty-three of us there and we went ahead with the workshop but, during the free time, we did healing work. One of the things I received on the journey was to look at what the terrorists did. Their brilliance was how they worked with their collective consciousness. It was the shadow side of spiritualism, saying you are a vehicle for the divine and for the Spirit. If you haven't done your work on your ego then you move into fanaticism, instead of being a real vehicle for the spirits. The veils between the worlds are starting to be thinner. There is an opportunity now to work on a deeper level for those people on a spiritual path, to be on a deeper level of cooperation with the spirits. My thought is that people have to look at what their desires are. What are their attachments to what they think is supposed to happen, instead of truly surrendering and being a true vehicle for the spirits?

Stop telling the spirits what you think you are supposed to be doing and say, "How can I be of service?" Come to a deeper place of humility. We are not humble in this culture; we are not humble in our spiritual practices. Many people take personal ownership for anything that goes right. You don't see this in indigenous cultures. There are more opportunities to work in a deeper spiritual way now. It is going to be challenging to see how people learn to move out of the way of their own egotistic desires. Can they stay humble and do the work at the same time?

JE: *How do you feel we can support humbleness in one another?*

SI: We have to keep looking at our motivations. Whenever we do anything spiritual or whenever we put anything out there in the world, it can come from a "what's in it for me?" attitude. We've been in a process of individuation. How can we let go of the "what's in it for me?" attitude? We can say we're going to be in service, unconditional service. Simultaneously, we need to follow our personal destiny. How do we take the awareness we've gotten out of the process of individuation, our own brilliance, our gifts, our strengths and be in service with them? How do we follow our destiny but work in a more collective fashion? We must start by working in community again, which people have been writing and talking about for awhile. It is time for people to work more on a community level.

Of course, the shadow side of that is those who band together from a place of fear and anger. How we can support each other is constantly remembering that fear is not the truth. When I was at the workshop the staff had asked me to lead a ceremony the morning of the tragedy. The security guard said to me two nights later when he saw me, "You know, I was ready to go out there and kill but, after the ceremony that you led, I wanted to sit down with these people and say, 'What's the problem? Just tell me. I'm interested in knowing'."

The challenge for everyone on a spiritual path right now is to move into a place of inspiration. We need to inspire people to keep our hearts open, instead of reverting to fear. In everything that we do, whether it is our writing or teaching, whether it's being with friends, we need to breathe through our hearts. Bring our energy from our heads to our hearts, experience breathing in love and light and breathing out love and light. We can make a difference being out in the world. It doesn't take many people collectively to shift the subconscious of the planet. How many people are willing to remember in the darkness what they learned in the light? Spiritual methods are great when everything is going great. For some people it is the first thing they tend to throw out the window when things get rough. It is so easy to be ungrounded. In shamanic cultures, shamans have been saying that we're dreaming the wrong dream.

One of the things I wrote this morning is about people who are willing to hold a good vision for the planet. No matter how bad things get, hold a vision of love and light and peace and harmony for the planet.

JE: *How can we encourage conscious visioning in a culture that is presently bankrupt of a vision for the future?*

SI: The people who do have a vision see doom and gloom. Watch the excitement when people get together and talk about doom and gloom. People's eyes light up and they get excited and they breathe fast. I wrote in *Medicine for the Earth* a line from Caroline Casey, a great astrologer. She says, "Imagination lays the tracks for the reality train to drive down." We must put out a vision and then surrender to "Thy will be done." We were born with these incredible imaginations. Everybody on the planet was born with God's gift of imagination, of being able to create and manifest. To me, this is why people are here. We have the creative potential of the source from which we came. We came here to learn how to manifest spirit being in body. Part of that is our imagination, our ability to really be able to vision. You can't vision without being able to stimulate the imagination.

Larry Dossey's work has been very courageous and brilliant in talking about how often-times doctors program their patients by giving them, "You have two weeks to live" or "You have six months to live." The patients follow exactly what they were told.

On that level, people hear something and take it in as a seed has been planted. Then a plant grows out of that. Think about what we are doing as a collective when we imagine that gloom and doom is coming. Conversely, if we don't imagine any vision, then we are open to the chaos surrounding us. Everything that manifests on the physical level begins on the spiritual level. As we don't remember this, we tend to create chaos. In my five-day soul retrieval workshop, we have been focusing on how to get people visioning and working with what they want to see for their present and future. The future is created from the present. As a people, we need to look at what will bring passion and meaning back into our lives again. When you are dealing with a lot of soul loss and you are disassociated, you don't notice how much pain there is in your life. You are too out of your body to really notice. But when you are in, if you had a successful soul retrieval and you're really in, you look at your life and say, "Wait a second. Something's not right here." In shamanic cultures, people knew their place in the community; they knew what their work was. In our culture it is different. People need help in being able to look at what would bring passion into their life again. What would help me thrive, instead of just survive? That is a crucial question. People have to consider this on a personal level and, especially right now, on a global level. I tell people that when we were in school we were taught how to not use our imaginations. We were taught how to conform, how to behave at certain levels. If you shine too brightly no one is going to love you.

Our societal programming made us see ourselves as small so that we would not get into trouble and we would be able to survive in our life. People really have to go back to that child-like state and remember how they imagined things, how they visioned as a child. Bring back the gift that everyone was born with - to be able to create. We're going to need to do that if we are not going to experience continual suffering.

JE: *One of the things I have been feeling in this time is the difference between transformation and transmutation. I felt very much in your book, "Medicine for the Earth", that you are really working with the energy of transmuting. Could you talk about how you came to that and what it actually means for you?*

SI: My book was stimulated by my desire to clean up the environment. I started journeying on this issue twenty years ago. There has been this underlying theme in my work of wanting to look at how we transmute, how we change the nature of toxic substances in our environment. I started journeying on it. Basically, the spirits were teaching me how to change myself.

If I were to say a sentence that describes *Medicine for the Earth,* it is who we become that changes the world, not what we do. For me, the whole point was trying to look at being able to transform on an inner level. I was just reading *Parabola*, the summer 2001 issue, which is all about "light." I was reading one of the articles the other day and there was a quote about alchemy.

Alchemy is the art of transmuting bodily consciousness into spirit. The quote is: "Body must be made spirit, say the alchemists, for spirit to become body." The principle of alchemy was not about turning lead into gold on a material level. It was about turning heavy, leaded consciousness into gold, light consciousness. We all have these golden seeds inside of ourselves and we need to let them grow. Alchemy is what I am talking about in transmutation, of being able to change what already exists, to change the nature of it into either a safe or a neutral substance. It could be a chemical in the outer world or it could be a state of consciousness inside of ourselves.

JE: *Where do you think we are going with soul retrieval work now?*

SI: I keep watching for what is going to happen to soul retrieval. There is still a real interest in it in this culture. It is definitely moving. It is exciting to see that it is still moving. On a mainstream level, shamanism itself has a limited place because, in the practice of shamanism, you have to believe in spirits. Something is missing and some forms of psychotherapy are not enough. People will still keep seeking out soul retrieval on a personal level because it is a spiritual part of what psychotherapy and traditional medicine can provide. You can't leave out the spiritual piece. We will be looking at how to bring back the soul of consciousness in a country.

We will be looking at how to bring back the soul of the land that has been traumatized. How to bring more soulfulness into our buildings and materials we are working with as people get sicker and sicker from what buildings are made of. I think soul retrieval is going to continue on a personal level but I think we are going to see it move into other areas.

JE: *You make a distinction between soul retrieval and soul remembering. Could you speak to that distinction, please?*

SI: It started out many years ago when I was doing a soul retrieval for a client. I had these parts to bring back and then my power animal said, "We have to go back to bring back what he has forgotten about himself, the gifts, the strengths and talents he came into this world to manifest." I said, "How did he lose them?" I am very auditory in my journeys so I have conversations with the spirits I work with. My power animal said, "He never lost them. He never lost this part of himself. It is something he has forgotten." And I said, "Well, if he has forgotten it how can we bring it back, if he hasn't lost it?" So he said, "We're going to go back before he was born and we are going to get him as he was coming into the world with this intention of living out this particular adventure this time around. And then, as he is coming back in, re-blow it back into him with the soul parts. I am teaching you how to do a soul remembering, instead of a soul retrieval."

The difference is that, in soul retrieval, we are looking for parts of ourselves that got lost because of trauma, whether the cause is emotional or physical. With soul remembering, it is more helping a person remember what has been buried inside of him. The nature of human beings is to project. When we are born, our parents and our teachers in school and society start to project a particular definition of who we are, what we're good at, what qualities we shine at. Those projections might not have anything to do with why you came into this world. I have worked with so many clients who were told by their parents at a young age that this is who you are going to be when you grow up. People follow someone else's plan but, then there's no passion behind it because it is a definition of themselves and it is a career that was chosen for them. The real question is, "What is it that I really came into this lifetime to do?"

JE: *Would you say that soul remembering is really touching into the soul's task or the soul's gifts it is bringing here?*

SI: Exactly.

JE: *How would you relate that in our culture? Is there a great deal of soul dismembering?*

SI: Absolutely, from a spiritual perspective. I don't know how many people are really in touch with what their life's purpose is. We allow ourselves to get distracted from that so early because we get drawn into "I have to do this and this and this" before I do anything spiritual. Where we are in society right now is that there are so many environmental stresses, political stresses and a lot of fear that constantly pull us out of ourselves. What would really be healing in our culture right now is for people to switch their priorities around. Look at what is my soul's purpose, why am I here, what are the gifts, talents and strengths that I came to share, how do I shine in the world? That would be a tremendous healing, but people get distracted from that too easily. I could see that this is a time where people would get distracted even more. One of the points of *"Medicine for the Earth"* is you can do your spiritual practice every day. How do we bring spiritual practices into our life on a moment-to-moment basis? When you bring spiritual practices into your life on a moment-to-moment basis, you start to tune into that part of yourself that has been forgotten.

JE: *Do you think that there is a feeling of despair that is holding us back?*

SI: Absolutely! Life without meaning equals despair. The level of depression and despair that we see in this country and I am sure globally, too, is staggering. If you think about it for a minute, all you have is your job and trying to pay your bills and that's it. If that is what life is all about, where's the joy? It's got to be more than a six-pack of beer on Friday night. So I think people are in a state of despair but they don't know it.

How we are dealing with it as a culture is to just give people drugs. I do believe that medication is needed with some people where there is a chemical imbalance but not on the wide scale level that antidepressants are being used. They are giving Prozac to little girls now. I think it is terrible because what we are doing is stamping out people's light even more. We are basically turning people into zombies, where people move into a state of despair and then they move into a state of numbness. How do we start dreaming a good vision of the future when people are numb?

JE: *How do you see the children and youth of our nation in this time?*

SI: I hear from parents and other people who are involved with children that kids are coming in with psychic ability, a spiritual ability, to move us. My fear is that these kids who are coming in with very strong psychic ability are going to be put on drugs. Are they going to be labeled A.D.D. and put on drugs that stamp out the abilities that they have come with to create change? I think it's going to be key right now to keep our kids inspired. When you look at young people today they are much more aware. They are coming in with a much greater consciousness than we have seen. I think they do have solutions. How do we keep them inspired or do we move them into the same place of despair that the rest of our culture is in?

JE: *I wonder if "despair" and "inspired' come from the same root? I just wrote the two words down. I like to play with words and what the actual feeling is behind the words.*

SI: When you look at inspired, for me what I think about is embers burning in the stove and we blow air on them to get that internal spiritual fire going. Despair dampens out that life fire.

JE: *Is there anything else you would like to talk about in terms of where you see us going with this work in the world?*

SI: Whenever I do an interview, the point I want to get across is that we need to start changing the story, not get so focused on what happened in the abuses of our past. Focus on what is a good vision for our present and our future. We have so much creative potential. Especially after we get back that lost essence and vitality from the soul retrieval, we have even more creative potential available to us. How do we get people inspired today to really be able to start to use their creative energy, to create a positive present and future for themselves, instead of the same abuses they have seen in the past? Spiritually, for those of us who are practitioners and teachers our real job is to inspire people right now. People are in despair and they are afraid. If we really want things to change we have to empower everybody. We have to get out of those hierarchical systems where somebody else has the power over us. Shamanism has been really brilliant in that through its thousands and thousands of years of existence. It has to do with direct revelation. The spirits are the authority.

If we don't do the ego work, then we start to bleed out our egos with what we think the spirits are saying. What we need to move to is not only to empower people but to get them to look at what the difference is between spirit and ego. We are not about saying, "I am going to run a plane into a huge tower because God told me to." Otherwise, we are going to see more of that, more fanaticism.

JE: *How much support does therapy have in the stages of transformation?*

SI: Therapy can be helpful, too. I have always turned to shamanism but some people have turned to therapy. Typically, in psychotherapy, once you have completed the issue you are working on you are terminated. Perhaps we should bring into therapy the thought of helping people look at, "Well, now that you have worked through that issue, how do you want to use your creative energy to create a positive present and future for yourself? What would bring passion and meaning back into your life again?" Typically, therapy does not go to that point. It deals with the problem. I am always asking the spirits to call me on my ego stuff. I am pretty honest with myself and I ask my friends to be honest too if they see me crossing the line. I am trying to move forward in the best way I can. Journeying is really good, psychotherapy is good, meditation, etc.--anything that gets people to look at themselves. Where journeying could be a problem is if people are trying to do a spiritual by-pass. Psychotherapy can be really useful in working through personal issues.

INTERVIEW WITH
ARIELLE GUTTMAN

September 20, 2001

Santa Fe, New Mexico

JE: *I am writing a book on the topics of soul loss and recovery, remembering ourselves. In your experience as a forecaster with astrology, was there energy in the world chart indicating the events of September 11, 2001?*

AG: Many people have asked this. I have put together the astrological chart information on the nature of the times we are in. I would say that the events exactly the way they transpired - hijacked planes crashing into the towers of the World Trade Center and the Pentagon and the plane crash in Pennsylvania - could not have been seen in the way it happened. But terrorism was an issue. Were open enemies of the United States ready to deal with us? Was our current political administration already focused on building up militarily and getting ready for war? Was a huge rift in the economy and the nature of life as we know it going to be happening? Yes. All of those things were indicated astrologically. I have been talking about them in lectures for the past year or so.

I focused on the inauguration chart of George W. Bush. So many people felt that this election was such a sham and so twisted. I had been looking at that. One thing to remember about the inauguration chart is that it is a set time, on a set date, every four years. No matter who would be taking the oath of office, you can't really change the nature of the time.

I look at the birth chart for the personal potentials. For example, one person is going to handle Mars energy in a different way than another person is going to handle Mars. Mars was highly angular in the inauguration chart this past January, 2001, meaning that the military was going to be built up in a significant way. With Mars very angular and Scorpio on the seventh house cusp at the moment of inauguration, the picture was of guns pointing to and from Washington. Big guns, to the rest of the world, being already on guard for something and all ready to respond quickly and efficiently. There were a lot of problems with that inauguration chart. It signified a time when the United States government and the values of the United States were being challenged in a very serious way. It is the time for a change. Many people, including myself, feel that the events of September 11 may very well catalyze a giant wake-up call for people who have been basically asleep or half asleep.

We all want to believe in a fairy tale world, we all want to believe in a planet of hope and peace and love and cooperation among all people but we have never envisioned, at least in this lifetime, a world like this. There always seems to be some war or some crisis or some conflict going on in a part of the world that is affecting the entire globe. How then do we change the collective mind out there? How do we transform it? That's the task we have at hand. That is what I am trying to brain-storm on right now with everybody. How do we get to Congress? How do we get to the leaders of the world? How do we stop the cycle of revenge?

He killed my brother so I am going to kill your brother, that's basically what the Middle East is doing. I just don't know how to do it and I would like to put the best minds of the world to that task. Let me ask you this because I know you are working on a really important subject right now. How does this tie in with the work you are doing? This is a collective soul loss and remembering that we are all going through.

JE: *That is one of the reasons I wanted to interview you. As an astrocartographer, have you looked at the forecast for the United States as a nation? Many of the interviewees for this book have been talking about soul loss of this country through addictions, materialism, to living through reason and will, rather than in a balanced way with our emotions as well as our spirituality. Soul loss in North America, and I would even venture to say in many, many parts of the world, is at epidemic proportions. How do we move from a state of dismemberment to access our true potential to shift into recovery? In what ways do we access our creative, inspired being and take action?*

AG: Those are great questions. The big picture is that the country is in a severely fractured state. The last election wouldn't have happened like it did, with such chaos, confusion and such a close finish, if we had a really clear choice, a vision, a leadership. What the country desperately needs right now is an enlightened leader, or at least an inspired leader.

Clinton was a brilliant statesman but he was a very poor role model. Could we trust him? Could we believe him? His personal life infringed too heavily on his public office which was really a shame because he had some really good ideas for the country and for the world. The current administration are not team players. They are very much focused on certain kinds of values which represent one part of America but not all of America and certainly not all of the world.

We are in the middle of a very intense Pluto/Saturn opposition right now. The whole world is. (I will speak to this later.) The astro cartography of this event (September 11, 2001), and the events in general of the day on the geodetic map, highlighted the planets Jupiter and Mercury. We equate Jupiter with Zeus, the benevolent gift-giver, the one who fills our Christmas stockings. How can we have Jupiter in this? But every planet has a shadow and herein lies the thing that we are really dealing with. The shadow of Jupiter is wealth and power and privilege, to the point where it becomes so greedy, so self-interested, so self-absorbed and so arrogant that it thinks of nobody else but itself. The enemy, whoever that enemy is, is attacking capitalistic greed, material wealth, arrogance, power and corporate greed. The corporate greed is affecting the rest of the world in a really detrimental way right now.

Think back on all of the protests that have gone on at the world summits over the last couple of years - Genoa, Seattle, Kyoto. Protesters' voices were silenced by police action. In these last protests the police were ordered to shoot them. What are we? We are supposed to be a free country. We are supposed to have the right to at least voice our opinion. Something that is not being listened to becomes shadow material. I see this in charts all the time. It is usually represented by Pluto but it can be represented by any planet that has a shadow. Anything that you deny becomes shadow material. When it becomes shadow material it comes at you in a very frightful way. It is the nature of what we are dealing with, the shadow of Jupiter. It is the boomerang effect. The corporate power structure represented by the two tallest building in the world, the twin towers of the World Trade Center in New York City, and the military might represented by the Pentagon are metaphors.

This is about governments and corporations meddling in the affairs of other countries, setting up and controlling other countries. They set up dictatorships and governments and regimes that go along with their plans to enhance the economy and to benefit their pocketbook at the expense of the environment, of indigenous people in other countries and their resources, their mineral wealth, their forests, their streams, the whole ecosystem.

Terrorism is to be abhorred in any form. It is not the solution. The solution is to open up dialogue to let all voices be heard. It is like the myth of the uninvited guest. At this huge banquet the thirteenth one is not invited because she would disturb the activities. "We want a party here, we don't want any opposition." The uninvited guest comes anyway and comes in a way that is even more destructive than if you had invited her.

JE: *How does Mercury impact the shadow side of Jupiter?*

AG: Mercury was there in a funny way. It was almost too humorous from a mythological point of view. Mercury is the god of air. Mercury was in Libra, an air sign. The attack was made from the air, from airplanes. Mercury is the god of travel, transportation, airports, and airplanes. There it was...the messenger! Mercury was in an exact trine and sextile with Pluto and Saturn, meaning the message could be delivered. Whoever picked the timing of this was brilliant. Mercury was in such a great aspect pattern to everything in the chart. It was as if an important message or a mission to be accomplished was aligned for operational success.

JE: *What about the Pluto/Saturn opposition in the world at this time?*

AG: That's a really interesting one. It is really overshadowing us. Three exact oppositions from Saturn to Pluto will take place between August 5, 2001 and the end of next May, 2002. In collective energy it is basically the idea of Saturn being the structure in the way we live, our security, keeping things the same. It also has to do with governments and tradition.

AG: Saturn is very traditional in "let's keep things status quo." Pluto comes along and says, "Let's change them." But the way Pluto comes along is not a knock on the door. "Hello, I'm here to help you change." Pluto says: "I'm going to blow this thing up because I don't like it." This is an interesting pairing. The last four or five periods in the 20th century of Pluto's pattern of opposition and conjunction, of tight intersection, heralded the beginning of World War I, World War II, the Great Depression, the end of World War II in 1947. That was one of the last big ones. Many of us were born at the end of that cycle. It was the beginning of the CIA and the beginning of the Cold War.

The next one was in the mid-sixties—protests, demonstrations, the Vietnam War. The last big Saturn/Pluto opposition of the mid-sixties brought up civil rights, women's issues, Viet Nam, equal opportunity, civil liberties. It all converged at that time. Now, that Saturn/Pluto opposition had a lot of help because Uranus was involved and Chiron was involved. Possibly all four of those planets were highlighted at that time and it took on some broader implications than the normal Saturn/Pluto opposition would. A normal Saturn/ Pluto opposition, from past events, means things aren't normal and don't stay the same. People are hanging on for dear life. Values and beliefs are questioned. Typically, something dramatic happens to change them.

JE: *Are there any other influences, such as Chiron, in this case from August 5, 2001 to May, 2002?*

AG: Not the way there has been in the past. This Saturn/Pluto one is pretty much on its own. Mars will affect it in the Spring of 2002. When Mars comes into play its energy actually escalates the enormity of very heated issues. On July 5th of this year we had a total lunar eclipse on the degree of the United States' Mid-heaven and opposite the United States' sun (the day after our birthday) and opposite George W. Bush's sun. So it was like a triple hit on the United States at that moment. In July of 2001, I remember talking about all three of those events coming up. I kept my eye on it, thinking that this was not the end of the story. I would have been very surprised if our country and our president had gotten through the rest of the year totally unscathed. These are big aspects. Eclipses occur in eighteen year cycles. Saturn/Pluto also occur in eighteen and thirty-six year cycles which, by the way, the eighteen/thirty-six year cycle with Saturn/Pluto is the nodal cycle, as well.

In a way it is very karmic. What wasn't handled in the last cycle builds up for eighteen years to be addressed in the next cycle. So that is what I think we are dealing with now.

JE: *In terms of soul consciousness, what do you believe our issues are?*

AG: For the country? We have a lot of shadow material. I have always felt "America the beautiful" and America the mighty and the strong and the powerful has a shadow image. We must address our shadow issues, especially around how we settled and occupied this country, in making reparations to the Native Americans. How we used slave importation and the sweat and blood of slaves to build our economy initially, I always felt we have never righted those wrongs. I don't know if we definitely have to pay reparations on a payment plan as such. I know our nation has never been able to stand up and say we are sorry. We can include leaders from both those groups to help us. They are the ones who helped build this nation; they are the ones who gave their ancestors' blood. We need a coalition of leadership. In the Native American cultures they have the medicine man and the elders and they all sit around in a council. Well, we have our council of senators and our council of congressmen but I am not sure that we are including all the different voices in them. One way that I think we could change is to call on those people and call on those spiritual leaders for advice and support. A third thing was brought up by Kay Cordell Whitaker when she did a bone divination right after September 11th. She gave us some of the information she had learned from the Hetakas, her teachers. It was the idea of putting the woman in the middle of the circle.

They put the female in the middle of the circle along with the children. The children come through the female, life is given through the female. The men surround the female in the center of the circle as protectors, but not just to go out and be the breadwinners and the women stay at home with the children - that's a part of their culture that is very important. It is not necessary that it would have to be done exactly that way here. The idea is that the women are in the middle of the circle and the women are honored, the feminine is honored. She was talking about the feminine/masculine in each one of us. We must put the feminine back in the middle of the circle. It touched us so much. We began to look around at leaders of the world, not just our government leaders, but corporate leaders and every facet of society, education leaders and so forth. If we were doing that as a family first and as a community and as a nation and as a world, I think we wouldn't be having nearly the problems we are having right now. The feminine would be looked to and addressed first. What is most important, is this being served? Then the feminine whose root is connected to Gaia, to the whole earth, would never condone some of the things that are going on from that position of consciousness. That doesn't prevent profits, it doesn't prevent people from getting wealthy, it doesn't prevent people from still having what they perceive they need to have in their lives. But it does it in a way that doesn't hurt anybody else. I think that is one of the most beautiful sentiments.

My companion, Jose, also offered another idea. We are going to put this on the Internet. It is the word "patriotic" which everybody is trying to use. "Be patriotic right now and wave the flag." "Patriotic" is from the Latin root meaning father. He suggests that we all be "matriotic," as it is mother earth that we live on. What we would like to do is wave the flag of Gaia, mother earth. We want to start this by hanging a flag outside of our door or hanging it on our car which has a picture of the earth on it.

JE: *In doing a forecast, do you see beneficial things coming into the chart of North America?*

AG: Yes, I do. We always have to look at the positive side of things. This crisis is going to fracture things in some ways. Think about the sixties as our last Saturn/Pluto opposition. It does bring people out to the streets again. It's a wake-up call for the civilian population that has been asleep. There are some really important things that we have to say and do right now. What impresses me greatly are the hundreds and even thousands of E-mails that have been coming in from everywhere. These E-mail lists have hundreds of names on them. I have received two or three that look like they've gone around the world three times and back again. It looks to me that we have a powerful network in place. From the signs of the times, Uranus and Aquarius, in a heartbeat these prayers and wonderful sentiments, powerful healing words and healing thoughts are going to everybody. That is the good news. The good news is that, in times of crisis, humankind gets to see the best of themselves. In times of collective crisis we stand up and do our part.

I feel there is going to be a lot of opposition. The Saturn/Pluto opposition is a lot of opposition to certain policies and the handling of things. Situations like this ultimately make people think twice about the way we want to develop our future. If anything, that's the healing we are going to get out of this.

JE: *Historically, it's at time of great conflicts like this that the next creative leaders are born.*

AG: My hope is that our next leaders will have done their own work, besides having great political ideas and being able to steer the country or the world in a certain direction. I think we all have to somehow confront our own demons and our own shadow material or it will come after us.

JE: *That's a very important point and it leads me to the next concept I wanted to talk about. Does soul loss or soul fragmentation, the shadow material, show up in a person's chart?*

AG: Yes, it does but it is not always easy to spot right away. I think this idea we were talking about earlier of projected material, denial of certain planetary archetypes or principles, shows up quite well. But the idea of soul loss is something different. I have looked at charts from the standpoint that this soul loss material may have happened to a person who carries it from another lifetime. But that begs the question. How does an individual get born into life or incarnate without a soul? Have you encountered that?

JE: *My understanding of soul loss is that our ancestral essence, which is our divine essence, is never breached. What is breached are aspects of ourselves, aspects of our spirit. We bring through life lessons that we may choose to step up to and work within during this time and this life. It is free will and free choice of the soul, in the soul's wisdom. The soul itself is infinite and can never be destroyed. It is part of the cosmos. When we individuate, it is the body soul that we are here to work with in the blueprint of our life lessons. Through our actions, thoughts, words, deeds, relationships are how our lessons keep coming up for us until we choose (or not choose) to work with them. I was wondering if those kind of pictures or potentials show up as oppositions or very strong aspects in an astrological chart?*

AG: Yes, they do. Probably the one planetary configuration that would speak more about soul than about mind, body or emotion is the north and south lunar nodes of the moon. The nodes were actually conceived of by the Chinese and Hindu astrologers as a giant dragon in the sky. The head of the dragon breathes the fire and is the forward evolutionary moving part of the dragon. The tail is the one that's releasing non-essential material. This is really ironic because it was the tail of the dragon (the material that it was excreting from the tail) that was sitting on top of the Washington, D.C. chart during this last inauguration in January, 2001. This gave me pause. It was very significant. There was a big dragon sitting on us. We've got a dragon to slay—to pay attention to (David and Goliath).

Everybody comes in with the nodes in their chart in some particular placement. What is interesting about the head and the tail of the dragon (and has been debated by astrologers for eons) is that some will look at the head of the dragon as being the place of the future and they look at the tail of the dragon as that which you need to leave behind, that which is not essential to your evolutionary pattern. However, I have a different take on it. My take is that the dragon is one body. If you are separating it you are cutting it off at the mid-section and splitting it off. Then you have accepted and rejected parts again, the split of consciousness personified in the dragon image, between body and soul.

JE: *In other words, in the split is separation?*

AG: Exactly. I think that the material you are bringing with you from before is actually material that could be quite helpful to you. When it becomes unconscious and habitual, you do not move forward. Because the nodes are in opposite signs in your chart and opposite houses, they have a balancing effect. If one gets slightly over-balanced or overweight, then the other one is going to feel the pressure and kind of tap you on the shoulder (or kick you in the rear) and say, "Wait a minute, you've got to pay attention to me, too." They have to be balanced. I think we have to be aware of the head and where we are going, and be aware of the obsessiveness of the tail—its creature comforts and additions—but we have to utilize them both in a way that they keep us sort of balanced and one-pointed.

JE: *Can you tell in a chart what the person's particular soul blueprint is saying to them?*

AG: I think if you look at the nodes by sign first, especially by sign is almost too universal. For example, somebody with the north node in Libra needs to work on developing relationships because the south node in Aries is where they have been too selfish in the past. Now they have to look into the other point of view. That's a very generalized way of putting it. I think also what will happen with the nodes is they will be conjunct to certain planets at birth, or oppose a certain planet, or square a certain planet. Those planets that are playing right into the nodal pattern of the birth chart give a clear message of what their soul came in to do. You look at all the different parts of that.

Individually, say there are no planets on the nodes and the nodes are just sort of hanging out there, which often happens. Through our lives there are transiting periods where planets transit over those nodes and give us an opportunity to work with an issue. Pluto, for instance, the slowest moving planet in our solar system, takes 248 years to go around the wheel. Nobody is going to live that long. Nobody is even going to make it half way through the cycle of Pluto in a lifetime. Pluto is moving faster now; it is in elliptical orbit. It's moving faster than it has ever moved. So people in our lifetime, in this period of time, are going to probably have Pluto moving about a third to a half of the way around the wheel by the time one incarnation cycle is complete. It is interesting to look at that from the standpoint of how Pluto is interacting with the nodal axis, because these are very big opportunities, moments in life where you have an opportunity to make some very big transformational processes.

JE: *Where are the nodes at this time?*

AG: They are in Cancer and Capricorn. There again, we are a Cancer country. They are sitting right on our country's chart right now. They were present for the inauguration, for the election, and for September 11.

JE: *What does this mean in laymen's terms?*

AG: The giant dragon was sitting upside down on our country at the moment of the inauguration. The chart of the inauguration we freeze as a moment in time and look at it as possible outcomes for the whole period (four years) as the way things might unfold. I think that there are some very big karmic implications for this cycle. There are some patterns that we are going to have to look at, for example at past actions. What is happening now is the result of past actions. They are tied together very strongly and one cannot be separated from the other. In other words, this has just not come out of the blue for no reason. What's happening now is for a specific reason, and we have to look at the issues. The actions of the past by the United States, by the government, by its leaders, by even the Bush family (it could get very personal here) have to be looked at as to the reasons of why this is happening. What we have to be careful of is having a perspective on this by the leaders of our country who can recognize that and not just say, "We're going to strike back. We're going to do something even worse than what they did to us." All that will do is perpetuate the cycle to continue for the next time the dragon comes to visit.

JE: *So in that way we would have missed the opportunity for the lesson or the soul recovery?*

AG: Exactly. People in their personal lives do this all the time. That is the one thing with astrology that I have not been able to determine with individual choice. When I see a pattern coming to a person, I see that there is an opportunity for them to address that issue or to go through the healing. But it doesn't always happen. They don't always choose to do it or they are not always capable of doing it.

That's where support therapies come in. We have to look at issues in a deeper way. Sometimes there is a rejection or a denial of issues. We're seeing this in our country right now. I don't think the leaders are looking. I'm hoping that they have advisors and some very smart people looking at this and advising them, saying, "Look, there is something else going on here that we have to look at." That would be my hope. Some spiritual leaders, some counselors, some advisors, some therapists, whatever it is they need.

JE: *I am wondering if spiritual nature shows up specifically in a chart?*

AG: Yes, there are definitely tendencies. I will look at a chart sometimes and immediately have the sense that this is a soul or spiritual being that has to keep being reminded that they have a body and that they are incarnated. There have been a lot of those who have come through. You also look at the very dense material bodies who have to be reminded that they also have a soul and there is a spiritual reason for them to be here, too. Which is also why I like the nodes because I think the nodes can help us balance both places.

JE: *How can the nodes contribute to our conscious awareness in balancing?*

AG: I think that the south node, which is so habitual and so familiar, is the remembrance of who we are and what we are here for. The north node can be very physical, how we express or manifest it into form. And yet I don't really feel that, until a person has their nodes balanced, they can be put into form in a really balanced way, in a way that works. I have clients who are celebrities, tied to that life, but they are feeling empty inside. They have millions of adoring fans out there but they go home at nights and are so lonely.

JE: *They are bankrupt.*

AG: Exactly. What is that? It's not anything from outside that can fill it.

JE: *It would be called soul loss from my traditional training. In the recovery or remembering we would work with our allies, our gifts, our talents hidden in this chart that we can call on. How can we access our gifts and talents?*

AG: I think we have to address the wound first. I just worked with a woman recently who has had a very successful, very fulfilling career in a certain field for twenty-five years, has made lots of money, has been widely successful, but still hasn't addressed her own wound. Somewhere along the line the fated intersection occurs. The nodal axis represents these fated moments in life. This country is at this fated intersection right now. You arrive at a fated intersection. In fairy tale and myth, this was called a crossroads. The young hero or heroine arrived at the crossroads. At the crossroads they met a magical old man or woman, or a magical little animal or fairy. Somebody from that magical realm could guide them to where they were going. It took them on this voyage where they may have had to battle with dragons and all kinds of things but eventually they were able to do it, to complete it successfully.

I think there is a deeper kind of awareness there. So when I am talking with people, initially everyone approaches me and I approach them on a very physical level, like, "Okay, how are things going in your life? This is what your chart is saying but how do you feel?"

You can usually tell right away whether or not they have handled it, whether or not they have gotten there, and whether or not they are even willing to go there. That is, of course, a very important thing. When a child's trust is betrayed, it creates a terrible rift (between body and soul). In fact, that's when many times I see the soul being lost. If we were going to talk about soul loss, a trauma, like sexual abuse, is when the soul is separated from the individual. It may take years for them to get it back, if they ever do

JE: *What would a person with soul loss look like in terms of a chart? Would you be able to spot it?*

AG: There are clues, certainly. There are so many different signatures in an astrological chart that it is hard to say. I would look at things like Pluto and I would look at things like possibly Mars and Pluto, or possibly Saturn, Mars and Pluto, those three combinations of planets interacting with the sun, the moon, the ascendant or the nodal axis in some particular way that would say, "Wow, this person has had a really rough beginning." Sometimes it will be confusing for them because they grew up in a home where Mum and Dad were both there; they were provided for really well on a material level. They had the best education, all the toys in the world, but there is a level of emotional, psychological or sexual abuse that has gone on which has really fractured the individual so that trust is just not there.

I have hundreds of examples in my files of different ways that pattern looks. It can look a lot of different ways. It comes up in every age group, at every moment, although the children that are being born now look really, really good. The last ten years or so, since the early nineties, children's charts look incredibly good as a whole. Even those children being born in the last ten years who are in difficult family situations have a spiritual kind of warriorship. They have a strength inside of them that they combat it in a way, or protect themselves in a way, that I think some of us didn't have growing up in past generations.

I'm not happy that our educational system is not addressing the needs of these children. Children today are dealing with things we never ever had to deal with. If I were ten years old I would be afraid to go to school today, not knowing whether there is going to be violence. Not only that, it's the violence in children, the violence in the world, the way it is escalating right into our own backyards right now.

JE: *This is an indication of massive soul loss. It's a way that we have forgotten ourselves that we live from a place of raw terror and violence.*

AG: I think our school systems and our education are failing. Children are simply not interested in going to school. They are not interested in learning because we are not addressing their needs right now. There are so many levels of society that need to change right now. This is not the vision of the new millennium that I think we had

There is a precursor to all of this. Everybody is living in fear following the events of September 11—fear of flying, fear of traveling, needing extra security systems, all of these things. Fear, fear, fear. We don't need to be living with more fear. That is not the vision of the new world, the twenty-first century, the new millennium that I think we had in mind for ourselves. You know, it always takes a really big event to change things. It always takes something really incredible. Maybe this is the incredible event that we can see will lead to the catalyzing change.

JE: *I feel astrology is an important science for our culture, to view the present and understand the past.*

AG: The general public is familiar with astrology from the standpoint of the prediction types of questions. What's going on now? Did you see this? I don't think people are always aware that astrology is something that is a really valuable healing tool until they have their charts done by a competent astrologer. It has a psychological component and a spiritual component that can lead to healing. I have been trying to focus more on where is the healing here? Is there healing needed and where is it? I only listen partially to what the person is saying. What's going on underneath? My work has also been with the soul at a different level, through the charts. Is this person living the kind of life that his soul wishes him to be living?

I really believe that we have all come here to live a joyful existence, that we don't have to live lives of denial and pain and suffering and oppression. I think it is a choice that becomes habitual if recycled around and around. As soon as they are shown a way not to recycle the story then I suggest a deeper therapeutic process if it is needed. This chart is an excellent way of examining that.

JE: *I believe the astrological chart is a clear snapshot of the soul's lessons and our potential and our gifts. The wound and the gift sit side by side. We are on the journey with a lot of support, many allies.*

AG: It's as if the astrologer can take the blood pressure, look at an EKG, or take a mammogram, something like that. Maybe not all astrologers are in the position where they can actually help to heal those things, but they can offer the next diagnosis or the next recommendation. It is a really good lens, a good eyepiece, in which to look at yourself. Every chart has a certain moment in time when you were born and every moment in time is good for something. Every moment in time created something. Some are more fractured than others and then there is more work to do. But every moment equates to a song, a musical note, something in the universe, a cosmic resonance. It says, "aha," this is *how* you live in harmony with the moment in which you were born!

July 31, 2004

Paterson, New Jersey

JE: *Can you tell the readers what Keetoowah means? And how the name relates to spirituality?*

SB: Keetoowah refers to the sacred Mother Mound, which is a physical location in the Appalachian Mountains. Spiritually traditional Keetoowah refer to this spot as the navel of the Earth, from which all our people come from.

JE: *Does the name Keetoowah mean anything?*

SB: Keetoowah refers to the Mother Mound and the people are called A-ni Ki-tu-hwa-gi.

JE: *Could you describe the beliefs of the Keetoowah people?*

SB: Membership in the Keetoowah is based upon family. In other-words, we are born Keetoowah. Keetoowah belief has always allowed intermarriage. We consider children of Keetoowah mothers to be full Cherokee. All Keetoowah are Cherokee, however, not all Cherokee belong to the Keetoowah faith. Our seven central beliefs are: 1) Honor the Creator; 2) All life is sacred and has spirit; 3) We are all equal; 4) Walk in balance with all creation; 5) The Earth is our Mother; 6) Honor the elders; 7) Walk in harmony with all creation.

Harmony is when you are in-sync with the internal and external environment. Balance is your place in the scheme of harmony. One must strive to be centered.

The **GA-TI-YO-I**, also called the Stomp Ground is the universal place of worship among all Keetoowah. During Ceremony it is consecrated land and it is a holy place.

JE: *What are the origins of the Keetoowah faith?*

SB: Keetoowah spirituality is from time immemorial and is one of the only faiths that is indigenous to North America. It is the oldest, uninterrupted, continuously practiced, faith in North America.

In 1889, The American Indian Religious Crimes Act took effect. It forbid American Indians to practice our faith. So, in the 1800's Keetoowah worshipers were forced to go into hiding and we became known as "**Nighthawk Keetoowah**", practicing our faith in the backcountry, in remote undisclosed locations. In the 1900's a separate "fire" was created from the Nighthawk Keetoowah fire and became know as the "**Nuyagi Keetoowah**". Both fires continue to exist today. In 1978, The American Indian Religious Freedom Act was passed by the U.S. Congress and signed by President Carter. The Act finally allowed Keetoowah families, who had hidden their religion and identities, to come out in the open. The Act was passed 191 years after the Continental Congress guaranteed this basic right for all other people.

JE: *Can you describe where Keetoowah people are from and a little about the culture?*

SB: Keetoowah are indigenous to the Appalachian summit region and have always been mountain people. The languages usually spoken are **A-ta-li** or **A-da-li**, (upper) **I-na-ge-(i)**, (wild), **O-ta-li** or **O-da-li** (mountain), **Ga-du-i** (top), **E-la-ti** (lower) or savannah and **Gi-du-wa** (middle) dialects.

Today Keetoowah dress like their non-Indian neighbors except during ceremonial times where the elder men wear a Stetson hat, white shirt and jeans. Women wear non-revealing clothing such as a Tear dress. It is customary for them to wear turtle shell shakers on their legs during the Stomp Dance. Traditional foods are served at ceremony.

Some famous Keetoowah are Dragging Canoe, Old Tassel, Bloody Fellow, Doublehead, Breath, Redbird Smith, Traveller Bird, Danawa Destoti, and Levi Gritts.

The Keetoowah have always been close to the Earth and with other Indians have given 75% of the staple foods to the world.

JE: *Would you speak more about the spiritual ways of the Keetoowah?*

SB: The Keetoowah are a Matriarchal Society. The children inherit their clan, their nationality, their community and their identity through the mother. Children belong to the mother's clan. The father is little more than a visitor. The uncle assumes the role of father in Keetoowah culture. The grandmother's brother and or the mother's brother is the father figure. The father, being of a different clan, is limited in his influence over the children. This is the way it has always been in spiritually traditional Keetoowah families. The spiritual and ceremonial leader of the Keetoowah is known as the **Di-da-hnv-wi-s-gi**. This person serves at the will of the Keetoowah Council and community. The **Di-da-hnv-wi-s-gi** is an honored and humble title. The position is a privilege and the person is in service to the community. The **Di-da-hnv-wi-s-gi** assists the Keetoowah Council with advice and suggestions. The Council consists of well respected, elected elders from the Keetoowah community. Traditionally oriented Keetoowah who are caring, giving, forgiving and faithful are considered the most spiritual.

The Keetoowah religious ceremonies usually last several days and are directed by a lunar calendar. The basic purpose of ceremonies is renewal. At the time of ceremony, traditional foods are prepared in traditional ways. All the "old" ways come to life during ceremonial time and traditions, customs and culture are passed down from generation to generation.

There are seven major holidays in a Keetoowah year: **Gi-la-go-di**, Spring New Moon, (March/April); **Se-lu Tsu-ni-gi-s-ti-s-ti,** Green Corn (August); **Do-na-go-hu-ni,** Ripe Corn (September); **Nu-wa-ti E-qua,** Great New Moon (September or October); **A-to-hu-na,** Friends Made (October/November); **E-la-wa-ta-le-gi,** Bush Feast (date varies); **U-ku,** Chief's Dance (every 7th year).

Keetoowah are the mound builders and we practice our ancient belief as it has been passed down to us. The **Ga-ti-yo-i,** the stomp ground is the primary place of worship. It must have a mound, water, fire and community. The worship consists of certain rites and rituals passed down from generation to generation. It is a living culture. It is customary to have a stomp dance during a ceremony. This is also an ancient ritual passed down through history.

All worship is learning traditional ways in order to be in harmony and balance in relation to one's own path, clan, family, community and nation.

JE: *Could you describe being out of balance or illness?*

SB: There are four ways that may cause illness among Keetoowah. These are: Fear, Jealousy, Anger and Grief /Sadness.

And there are ways to help prevent illness among Keetoowah. These are: Balance, Harmony, Cooperation and Inclusiveness. Being in total Harmony and Balance with all of creation is a way to prevent illness. To achieve this, one must also be centered. One must understand their place in the scheme of all creation and strive to maintain that place.

JE: *Do you have any frame of reference for spirit illness? What are the symptoms of disharmony?*

SB: An individual who is rude or angry are two examples of being out of balance and therefore not in harmony. Physical illness is a direct result of being out of balance. When you are in harmony with all creation there is no place for illness to enter. One's personal behavior will dictate whether that individual is in balance and harmony. Non-verbal behavior is also another indicator of disharmony. For example, someone who looks distraught or someone who is extremely violent may reflect disharmony in their body language.

A Keetoowah may choose to address disharmony in their life in one of two ways. The first being communally, at ceremony where one can re-enforce their beliefs. The second way is privately. One can make prayers or request to have personal time with the **Di-da-hnv-wi-s-gi.**

JE: *Do you feel Keetoowah beliefs have relevance for our contemporary world?*

SB: Keetoowah beliefs are infinite and have no beginning or ending. Our beliefs are as relevant today as they have been for thousands of years. Our beliefs are reflected in our values and how we conduct ourselves. For example, we value cooperation rather than competition; group rather than individual emphasis; modesty rather than self-attention; non-interference rather than interference; patience rather than aggressiveness; non-materialistic rather than materialistic emphasis; orientation to the present rather than use every minute and orient towards the future; respect for our elders and age rather than emphasis for youth; harmony with nature rather than the conquest of nature; religion as a way of life rather than religion as a segment of life; spiritual-mystical reverence rather than skepticism; non-verbal communication rather than verbal communication; personal caution rather than personal openness; listening and observation skills rather than verbal skills; extended family is important rather than emphasis on the nuclear family; no eye to eye contact rather than the importance of eye to eye contact in the dominant culture; cultural pluralist rather than assimilation imperative. The conflict in values with the dominant culture may create stress, anxiety and frustration among Keetoowah and is known as Post-Colonial Stress Disharmony.

JE: *Is there anything else you would like to share with us?*

SB: A person must first know who they are and their own history and culture. Only then can a person seek their place in their culture. Keetoowah is a way of life, not a segment of life. We do not proselytize. We are bound by our covenant not to be political.

Places you may wish to visit are; Nighthawk Keetoowah at Stokes Stomp Ground in Oklahoma or the Nuyagi Keetoowah at Stokes Stomp Ground in New Jersey.

JE: *Any final words of wisdom?*

SB: Keetoowah elders often say, "Listen, or your tongue will make you deaf."

INTERVIEW WITH
JUDITH SCHMIDT

November 23, 2001

Goldens Bridge, New York

JE: *How did you become interested in the use of imagery in healing? When were you first introduced to it?*

JS: It was 1980 I had heard from an old friend of mine that there was a teacher in Jerusalem whose name is Collette Muscat. I was told by this friend that Collette did something that is called "waking dream" therapy. This friend felt that I would be very drawn to this way of working. At that time, I had gotten my doctoral degree in 1975; and when I came back to New York from California where I had done my doctoral work, I became involved with the Core Energetics Institute. So it was from 1975 until about 1980—it was probably 1980 that I went to Jerusalem. I went there and had a private meeting with Collette and experienced imaginal work. I said to myself, "I am home." You know that soul feeling; this is where I live, in this space. At the time I had been involved at the Core Energetics Institute which was a very different way of working. I still, to this day, find the ability to read a body, to read the structure of a body very helpful, but I no longer do Core Energetics work. I work, rather, with the energy of the images. From that time on, I took several trips back to Jerusalem and continued to study with Collette. Out of that work really evolved my own way of doing imagery which is in many ways connected to the sensory body. I have taken my lineage from Collette and my lineage from John Pierrokas and very much made them my own.

I don't any longer work in the way I was taught to work by either John Pierrokas or Collette. Collette prefers to work by doing very short, what she calls "shock" imagery, where it will shock the whole system by presenting an imaginal exercise. I will sometimes do that for somebody who is in, let's say, a very dire situation and they can't find their own way in. The system really does need to be shocked. My preferred way of working now is for somebody to enter their own sensory experience, their own sensory pathways, and to find their way into imaginal space and time. There they meet what is unknown to them and open new possibilities. I use the way I was taught as a foundation and find my own way, and I feel very grateful to my lineage.

JE: *When you say that this helps someone meet what has been unknown to them: How does the imagery help a client open these pathways or these sensory doorways?*

JS: I work longer than a single session. I find that if you are going to enter imaginal realms you need space and time that is longer than a fifty -minute session. I prefer to work a double-session or at least a session-and-a-half. During that time, somebody may, for example, tell me about what is happening in their lives. Most often in the telling, there is a re-telling of a very old story, a story that is in a rut that causes suffering. The rut itself is what causes suffering.

As I am listening to the person talk to me, I tend to listen for two things. I tend to listen for the image that the person is expressing without even being aware of it. For example, today somebody said to me, "I am at a loss. I am at such a terrible loss." Now I will hear that as an image so that when I have completed the cycle of listening, I will tell the person, "I heard you say before that you are at a terrible loss. I wonder if you could close your eyes and find yourself at that loss--to feel yourself, to be there at that loss, to see who you are, to sense everything about this place." Imagery is not just about seeing. That would be more visualization. Imagery really involves every one of the senses. So I would invite that person to see, hear, feel, taste the atmosphere of that place where they are at a loss. Let's say the person will tend to be very quiet for quite awhile and you can see that there can even be rapid eye movement. You know by the body language, by the eye movement, by the facial expression that the person is crossing a threshold from the old story into a more open space where they meet themselves, but the self that has been unarticulated heretofore. Let's say that person will say (there might be tears), "I am at a place. This place of loss is rubble; it is a bombed-out place." This is exactly the experience I had with somebody today. "It's a bombed out place after a war and everything is in ruins and I am the only survivor."

To me, when a person can begin to weave their story in imaginal space, I can feel in my own body that they are lending their story a certain kind of nobility. A certain kind of deep dignity because there is a freshness and an aliveness, even to this bombed out place. There is universality. There is an existential depth that they can feel about their life. You can feel it in the listening and the witnessing. Then I will ask the person, "How does it feel in your body, in your breathing? What is it like to breathe in this rubble? What is the taste?" So they really become grounded in this space which, again, to my way of thinking, becomes as real as physical space. It has all of the palpation and pulsation, all of the aliveness, and the absolutely unknown possibility. Whereas in the story that goes round and round, there is really no possibility. If you go exploring this rubble, what do you see? One of the things I experience, Jane, which is really sacred to me in doing imaginal work (there is only one person I have worked with in twenty-five years now where this has not happened) is that something turns. When you take the energy all the way in, in its despair, its darkness, something turns. So when this woman searches in the rubble she finds a bird with broken wings. It's still alive. It was very powerful to witness to this. What she did was she took the bird and put it next to her heart. Her heart became the respirator for this bird. Again, in imaginal work there is no interpretation that this bird is a wounded soul. There is no reducing anything. Everything is utterly what it is--no analysis, no interpretation, just the knowing at this level of the psyche that this discovery is transformative.

JE: *When an insight or a profound situation which you have just described arises, how does the client integrate that into their life?*

JS: For this particular woman it reactivated a prior loss for her, the sudden death of her husband. The grief that came up was very identified with the grief of September 11th. So when she finds this bird, there are two possibilities. As imagery surfaces, I feel like there are two ways to relate. One is to have the faith that something is going to incubate in this person's healing process, in this person's own inner healer. The image will become part of the internal healing process. The other is to activate the healing image into external life. I think it is very critical to know when to allow something to incubate and when to take it out and practice it.

JE: *How would you differentiate that?*

JS: For example, this person carrying a bird with a broken wing says, "I am carrying that bird next to my heart and my heart is its respirator." If that person is sitting in the session wearing a shawl around her shoulders, I will take that as an opportunity to try to bring what is deeply in imaginal space somewhere into physical space. So I will say, "Is that bird next to your heart under anything?" I won't even ask explicitly if it is her shawl.

But she did say, "Yes, it's under my shawl." So then I say to her, "Well, you know, if you go through this week, no matter what you are doing, no matter where you are, no matter waking or sleeping, the very deepest depth of you is carrying this bird under your shawl. What you can do if you wish to is several times a day look and see how this bird is. Look and see what has happened to this bird. Be aware of your heart beating as the respirator for its heart."

So, it's a kind of practice that takes the person into the internal state but externalizes it. Sometimes I won't give any practice. I will just say, "In the deepest part of you, this is happening. You don't have to do anything. This is going on inside of you, even when you are driving your car, eating your dinner, it doesn't matter." Now what happened with this woman when she came back today was that the broken-winged bird was no longer a bird. It had become a wounded angel and a very particular angel. This is what the psyche will do when it has its own autonomous life.

To answer your question, to give that kind of practice that wasn't right out in the world helped her to keep the transformation going in a kind of transitional space and then she will look after the world in a very big way.

JE: *So incredibly archetypal.*

JS: Yes, to me that is the opportunity and the imaginal space. Again, to be able to retell your story in a different way than what is very up close and personal, it begins to take on a larger archetypal meaning that is both personal and impersonal that is collective. For me, when I feel that happen, it makes one's life part of the large nobility of life. It helps one hold one's life in a way that can be felt as sacred.

JE: *It feels very "freeing", what this woman created within herself.*

JS: I think that happens in the context of a trusted, inter-personal relationship, that one can journey.

JE: *Are you saying in terms of the therapeutic relationship that the support is there?*

JS: Right. I know I have found in my own personal therapeutic relationships when I have been in therapy that there is either a focus exclusively on the inter-personal relationship or a focus on my history.

Very seldom is there the integration of all the levels of existence which is inter-personal relationship, archetypal relationship, and relationship to one's personal history.

JE.   *Judith, what is your sense of the difference between fantasy, which is so not what we are talking about?*

JS: I would call myself an imagery therapist. I have background in object relations, in waking dream work, and certainly an interest in Jungian work. I am well grounded in it, but I am not certified as a Jungian therapist.

Fantasy is an escape from reality, a withdrawal from reality. It is an abortive attempt to enter what imagery leads one to, but it doesn't go there. In imagery, very often you will have to go through a dark space to get to a healing space. In fantasy, you bypass dark places and you make yourself feel better by repetitively going to a place that feels good. I am thinking of "The Secret Life of Walter Mitty" or let's say somebody who uses the Internet and never meets anybody but uses it for relationships. They can build all kind of relationships that are based on fantasy. So they go round and round, they are recycled over and over again, but they don't meet any transformation. I think they have a very different intention. I think the intention of fantasy is to feel better. The intention of imaginal journeying is to journey, to discover, to open possibilities. It's not the intention of fantasy.

JE: *I've always felt that fantasy has its own agenda with a beginning, a middle, and an end. It has always felt false to me but I have never been able to really find the language. When you say "intention"...*

JS: I don't mean conscious intention. The need that it grows out of feels like a substitute for something that is missing in one's life - it is compensatory.

JE: *Judith, are you aware of the Shamanic term that is known as "journeying"?*

JS: Yes, I have worked with several people who have studied with Harner so I have some familiarity. But if you want to spell it out for me please do.

JE: *I will just briefly say that, from the Shamanic perspective, you can teach the client to journey. Also the counselor can journey on behalf of a client..*

JS: Oh, to journey for them. Right.

JE: *You can do that or you can teach the client to journey on their own behalf which is my preferred method; assisting the client in and out of what you are calling these spaces or realms (Michael Harner calls them "non-ordinary reality").*

JS: I would call them "non-deterministic realities". They are not determined by personal history.

JE: *For example: Journeying to the spirit world for soul retrieval is to go in support of someone who is untrained, doesn't know how to access these realms yet, and to actually bring back a lost part of the soul*

JS: Yes, I am aware of several people I work with who told me about this soul retrieval. In fact, I have done a soul retrieval - someone has done one with me.

JE: *What was your experience like?*

JS: I'll tell you. This is a bias of mine, Jane. I don't quite understand this about myself but I have a very deep bias, deep preference, if I am finding the right word. It has something to do with the word "sacred". I have such a deep sense that what lies behind the veil in a person's consciousness should only be opened by their own soul. I don't know what that's about but it is so deep in me that I feel I can't resonate to anybody else's doing that. So when I experienced that myself I found it interesting but I can't even remember what was told to me. I don't know what that is. I am not saying it is right or wrong. I'm really just owning it as my own experience. People have reported to me their soul retrieval experiences and have experienced it as very powerful.

JE: *I feel there is such strength and strengthening of the soul's resonance in finding its own path. In a sense I really agree with you. It's a wonderful way to work. I work both ways with clients but the most rewarding way for me is to have the client be able to access and find their own soul. I actually find an increased frequency of their life force when they access it on their own with very little outside help. Obviously, there is basic support and cooperation together. In shamanism it is the spirits that do the work and bring the soul part to the person; and then it is the person who accesses their returned soul in a powerful way.*

JS: When you were describing the Shamanistic journeying, what was coming to me was my own connection to the Kabalistic understanding. The Kabalah says the soul has two roots. One root is connected to the physical form, physical history, physical life. Then there is an upper root to the soul that is connected to the invisible. When I can be a guide to somebody who is journeying, I feel they are connected to the upper soul root, to the hidden realm that is creating us. I don't know how that lines-up with shamanistic understanding.

JE: *It is actually very parallel. In the Shamanic practices and in the cultural anthropology that I have been reading and studying, there is the body soul which has the root in the physical world. Then there is something in many indigenous cultures which is known as the "free-soul." That is the infinite soul, the infinite aspect of our essence. So when you mention that from the Kabalah it is wonderful to have that comparison because I hadn't run across that.*

JS: In a certain branch of Buddhism (which it will come to me; I forget the name right now.) they call it "other power".

JE: *Other power? Because in Buddhism, per se, there is no thing as "soul" or "soulness".*

JS: No, but there is emptiness, what they call *shinyata* which carries all potential. If you can connect beyond the physical root, then you can be affected by this undifferentiated life energy.

JE: *There really is, in many different cultures, the opening of the mystical within us.*

JS: Yes. You are speaking about reading, Jane, are you familiar with *The Spell of the Sensuous?*_

JE: *No.*

JS: It is an incredible book, written by a man by the name of Abram. He talks a lot about indigenous people and basically what he is talking about, what moved me so much about this book, is unity of the sensuous and the mystical. The sensuous is the doorway to the mystical. You will love this book. That's what I find in doing imaginal work that if you enter through the senses it is a paradox. If you enter through the senses you connect with what infuses the senses.

JE: *And in that connection it feels as if there was tremendous life force. In your practice, Judith, do you exclusively use imagery as the foundation?*

JS: I would say that imagery is the centerpiece, the cornerstone, but I move in a back and forth rhythm between I and Thou, the outer I and Thou (the client and myself), and then the inner I and Thou which is the client's I with the Thouness of creative life force, a very intimate relationship. And then the movement into one's good life outside of the session. There is a kind of balance when I work with somebody, so there is a "presencing" for each of those parts of being.

It takes first place so that the crucible in which we are working is always in good preparation. If there is anything that needs focusing upon, I feel it is my responsibility to bring that focus and then the person is prepared to journey. It is that kind of rhythm.

JE: *It feels like a sacred dance.*

JS: And then there are times when a person will do many, many sessions of imagery work. They can go six sessions with, say, just journeying and then you see something begin to unfold into their lives because the journeying has prepared that. Let me see if I can give you an example.

I am thinking, for example, of a woman who lost her husband, her kids, her home, her marriage, all at the same time. Everything was gone after thirty-five years of foundation. When she came to me she could barely walk, she was in such panic at being uprooted. At one point she felt herself to be on a bridge and there was the image. So I asked her to close her eyes and see what kind of bridge she was on. It was a Tibetan bridge. I had never heard of a Tibetan bridge but when she described it to me I could really feel the precariousness of her being on this bridge which was made of rope over this horrendous chasm. In the imagery, she was just holding on, clawing her way across because the winds and the storm are blowing this bridge. Through the imagery she is creating a holding environment for her terror. In crossing this bridge she is finding her sheer panic. When she comes to the other side of the bridge there is a bed of leaves and she just lies down there.

When she comes back for the next session she's in the bed of leaves. Two weeks later her husband came to take their bed because he had chosen it when they were separating their belongings. She came to me and said, "You know, Judith, I am not ready to buy a new bed. I am sleeping on a mattress on the floor. Nobody has ever slept on this mattress. It is my bed of leaves. For the first time in my life I am sleeping on my own space. I always slept on somebody else's bed." That, to me, was the beginning of a whole movement to make her alive.

JE: *What an incredible arising for her and the way in which the insight came to her!*

JS: Exactly. See, there was no interpretation. Somebody once said to me, and I have never forgotten it, it was a kind of paraphrasing of a poem: "Don't talk apart what is whole in the heart." Imagery has a wholeness to it. No interpretation, don't talk about it. It has its own wholeness, its own holiness, and its own healing. So when I hear an image like that I put my hands together and say, "Thank you, God."

JE: *It is immediate.*

JS: Of course, I don't think doing imagery is for everybody. I don't know how it works in shamanism, but I don't know if it's everybody's way, either as the healer/therapist or as the client, to go the paths of imagery. I am not sure.

JE: *It is almost a misnomer, the word "imagery" because there is so much else in the sensate realms that are part of this.*

JS: Yes, that is true. What I prefer to call it is "soul journeying". It is soul therapy.

JE: *This has been very wonderful. Is there anything else you would like to say? I could just listen to you forever.*

JS: I don't think so. I just hope I have been of help to you.

JE: *You have been wonderful and generous.*

JS: Interesting, because when I wrote my book I interviewed several people, and it was nice to see that I can do that for someone else. And the circle goes round.

Chapter 4

Soul Loss and Recovery, NOW
(A Post-Modern Perspective)

Sweet Darkness

When your eyes are tired
the world is tired also.

When your vision has gone
no part of the world can find you.

Time to go into the dark
where the night has eyes
to recognize its own.

There you can be sure
you are not beyond love.

The dark will be your womb
tonight.

The night will give you a horizon
further than you can see.

You must learn one thing.
The world was made to be free in.

Give up all the other worlds
except the one to which you belong.

Sometimes it takes darkness and the sweet
confinement of your aloneness
to learn

anything or anyone
that does not bring you alive

is too small for you.

(Whyte 1998, 23)

Soul loss has levels and layers of forgotten aspects of the soul. These forgotten aspects have fragmented away from the soul and are frozen in space. Some symptoms, relating to profound moments in a person's life, are more pronounced. Other indications of soul loss may relate to a repeating behavioral pattern such as "giving-away" one's power to someone considered to be in authority. This behavior might also include abdicating self-responsible choice. For example, in our culture we have been taught to depend upon the corporation that employs us to also look after us. We abide by corporate policies and have been taught to be compliant and non-inquisitive even if we are uncomfortable with those policies. Giving away power to outside sources can be subtle and over time seemingly painless; however, becoming "leaky" in this way can establish a long-term behavioral pattern of soul loss until something happens in life to awaken us.

One recent example in which we are witnessing tremendous soul loss is with many corporate conglomerates' takeover of other companies coupled with our country's current state of economic recession. Many highly-skilled people are being "given the package" or are being laid off in North America. For anyone who identifies self esteem or personal value through career or job, this kind of loss can be shocking; and if the shock, anger, depression, and fear states are deep enough, soul loss will result. A sense of disbelief and frozenness may follow for many unemployed. Grief for the loss which is so unacceptable in our culture gets stuffed away. People are told to "buck up and get over it." But a culture that has been trained and encouraged to base self-worth, ego and identity on career or job will experience a huge amount of soul loss with very little to no spiritual support available to process and find creative alternatives for right livelihood.

Loss of a job or career can also cause deep soul loss resulting from the fear that arises in an individual and in groups of people whose lives and survival are suddenly in question. The fear, anxiety, and self esteem issues are even more poignant with the trauma of losing a home and the consequences to family welfare. The stress level being experienced by many hundreds of thousands of people in the United States, as reported in our news media everyday from losing a steady income is destabilizing, shocking and depressing. Soul loss and soul recovery can be a healing way which factors into inspiring people to find creative solutions and to reevaluate their lives and work. This healing way brings spirituality into the work we choose to do.

I recently counseled a middle-aged woman who had been given "the package" after 20 years of dedication to her company in a corporate buy-out situation. She wanted to check on the company policies regarding human resources, job search and re-training. When she accessed the human resources manual file on her desk computer, the entire company policy manual had been removed, not only from her terminal but from every other employee's as well—a company-wide sweep. No one in the company could review the "rules and regs" on how they were being treated according to policy or what support systems were available to them in order to process the shock they were experiencing. The human resource team of professionals was not returning calls and had themselves been short-listed and summarily let go with only two week's notice. My client felt violated, angry and scared. After twenty years of identifying with her career and doing good work in the world, she was struggling with severe depression, fear, grief and profound soul loss. She is only one example. Fortunately, she had a foundation in spiritual practice and turned to this for support in her time of grieving processing and sorting through her feelings and reviewing her life.

Soul loss can manifest emotionally, mentally, physically, and through becoming dispirited on many levels. Symptoms are wide and varied and much more prevalent in our culture than has heretofore been recognized. The disconnection of the soul from its indigenous nature along with its deep sense of being interrelated to all sentient life and the spirit world has resulted in a profound state of forgetting our true ancestry in our culture. We have lost the sense of inner power and what it means to be filled on the inside with the soul's ancestral heritage—known shamanically as "The Song." This disconnectedness has caused us to become weakened spiritually and our energy field is perforated.

Listed below are life experience factors that can relate to soul loss. Many of these symptoms are interrelated, and one may not be the sole cause. Again, please note that not all of these conditions will result in soul loss, but can, if support and spiritual assistance is lacking.

- chronic depression with or without clinical diagnosis
- chronic illness (such as Chronic Fatigue Syndrome—CFS)
- suicidal tendencies and attempted suicides
- chronic chaos (connected world-wide and/or individually)
- living from crisis-to-crisis

- spiritual intrusion (i.e., religious indoctrination in forced and rigid terms; also ghost attachments and possessing entities from the unquiet dead)
- repeating self-destructive behaviors (recycling)
- anger/rage unexplored and acted out or acted inwardly in negative patterns
- trauma—mental, physical, emotional, spiritual
- abuses (all forms)
- addictions (all types of chemical abuses, consumerism, materialism, gambling, etc.)
- soul loss from a loved one's death
- coma
- accidents
- surgeries
- acrimonious divorce
- loss of job, career loss
- terrorism (i.e., Oklahoma city bombing, "9/11" terrorist attacks)
- war—post-traumatic shock
- unexplored anxiety and stress over extended periods of time
- natural disasters (floods, tornadoes, fires, landslides, etc.)
- birth trauma (fetal alcohol syndrome, crack babies, any birth traumas mother-to-child)
- genetic soul loss through lineage or ancestral patterns (i.e., child abandoned by alcoholic parent, child becomes an alcoholic)
- all forms of dissociative behavioral disorders

- psychic invasion (ET, cult abuses, power-over control, invasive brain washing, mind control)
- chronically giving away power to outside sources (the inability to reference self and be self-responsible) also known as being "leaky"
- global policies country-to-country based on power, greed and control (i.e., buying another country's resources, raping the land)

Not all of the listed symptoms or experiences cause soul loss. For example, a surgery with an honest doctor-patient relationship coupled with the patient's support factors such as family, hospital care, and post-operative therapies can contribute to a healing experience. Trauma can be avoided. Soul loss relates to specific factors being in place and is individual to each person's life experience. It also relates to the larger context on a worldwide level of soul loss through, for example, the denigration of natural resources and pollution of the earth.

Soul Fragmentation or Soul Loss and the Anatomy of the Energetic Dimensions

There are levels to the seriousness of soul loss. There are characteristics in the human energy field that can contribute to fragmentation. The aura is the energy body that supports the physical, mental, emotional, and spiritual bodies. Since childhood, I have seen the energy lights around and inside a person and also in places on the earth such as energy vortices. The word *chakra* literally means "intersection" in Sanskrit, "wheel" or "disk" (Fox 1999, 94). I have been taught energy medicine both by my indigenous elders and, in a more Westernized way, by healers who taught the laying-on-of-hands. My initial training in energy medicine began specifically in 1978 when I became an apprentice to Tuguk, an Inuit Shaman (see Introduction – Part I). What follows are my perceptions and experiences in working with the inter-dynamics of the physical, emotional, mental and spiritual energies. Chakras, or energy centers, metabolize and keep the energy field in balance. I observe cords in each chakra that relate to life experiences, all forms of relationship, country of birth, present home, and grounded-ness (to name only a few). These cords are tensile connections with great flexibility and strength. They represent both present experience and past history. When a cord is withdrawn, broken, or sluggish (i.e., blocked), the potential functioning ability of the charka becomes weakened. For example, the first three charkas relate to the immediate human condition as I perceive them. Life force flows from the earth and the environment into the first (or root) chakra, and from the person back into the earth and environment. It is a circuit not unlike electricity. Resonance is passed back and forth between every living being. Resonance is like a tuning fork with sound, color, clarity, texture, feeling, and emotion. Each living being has a resonance and, while some resonances appear or are experienced on a specific basis, each individual within the species has its own unique blueprint (or song). For example, deer as a nation have an overall resonance, but each deer in a herd has his/her specific "hoof print" characteristic to it and none of the others within the species. The same principle applies for rocks, trees, the human species, and for all life.

When a chakra's resonance becomes unbalanced, the overall metabolism of the entire energy field is less strong than if it were operating on "all eight cylinders." Chakras can be compared to the image of a Russian nesting doll—one charka interconnects within the other, and the other, and the other all the way out to the edge of the energy field and beyond the individual life form to connect energetically with all other life forms. Imagine this for a moment. We are all interconnected and touching, co-mingling and sharing life force continually with waves of energy coming and going faster than the speed of light. This energetic exchange is the true way of being interconnected, being one.

What affects one charka has an interconnected effect on the entire energy system of an individual. When a charka is compromised through some form of shock or trauma in a life-altering event, the energy vortex and its cords can appear torn, dark, muddy, wobbly, sluggish, disengaged. Fortunately, all life forms are tough nuts to crack or we would not have made it through millennia of evolution, disaster, war, and famine. Life has transcended in a creative way, picked itself up, dusted itself off and gone forward. But it has done so with the imprint of the past in our "soulular" memory as the way things should proceed. What has been missing is the rebalancing of spiritual knowing and wisdom in the physical world.

However, if an energy system is traumatized and goes out of balance, something else happens: repair, rebalancing and harmony does not take place. Instead a hole exists. It exists in the energy field and, like the Russian nesting doll, goes deeper into the home of the soul, into the blueprint of existence.

The line of the soul has been named *hara* an ancient Japanese word meaning "belly or center of being" (*New World,* 3rd ed., s.v. "hara"). The soul's line or hara is a multifaceted energy body unto itself. The soul line is holographic, appearing in every cell of our human bodies as DNA. On this level the soul line or conscious spiritual blueprint is alive. "Soulular" and cellular experiences are interconnected with all consciousness. The hara and the cellular DNA are holographic and relate to the infinite soul as it is expressed in physical form.

In shamanic terminology the soul line appears as a double-headed serpent. Indigenous traditions have represented this as Quetzalcoatl, Kundalini, the snake in a circle or double helix pattern (Narby 1998, 92-3). The holographic energy of cellular and "soulular" knowledge appears in DNA as lines of amino acids, like a zipper, connecting, disconnecting, reforming, and always moving. In Narby's research, indigenous traditions have also experienced this as the line of remembering the soul, the soul's purpose and task, or ancestral remembering of wholeness (ibid., 160).

Where a rip or tear appears in the soul line and, in some cases, in the human energy field, there can be soul loss. Soul loss appears as a broken circuit, a filament that leaves the overall soul line and dangles in space. On the hara a dark dot or break is experienced like an exclamation point on a dark hole. The overall soul line nests within the energy field within the human and also in all beings. The soul line appears as a beautiful blue white column running through the being. When there is soul loss, punctuation points appear or disengaged filaments dangle in space indicating dark points of departure. In fact, these points are points of splitting off. When tracked back into the charka system, the leaky or under-metabolizing chakra will appear in a dysfunctional manner, dark or torn like the webbing of life or a screen door that has been ripped open.

In a healthy soul line, the blue-white column is shimmering, vibrating with life force like the twinkling stars in a clear night sky. The soul line is connected to the infinite, the divine soul. Following the infinite soul line outward connects us to the very moment of conception and beyond to the majestic interrelatedness of all life.

Moving into the human condition (and also all other life forms upon this earth), we can track the soul line into a personal resonance. This resonance or blueprint is anchored within each physical, emotional, mental, and spiritual body. In humans it first appears about four feet above the crown of the head in an arch of silver and golden light. The arch appears as a halo or a fully rounded disc of light as is so often depicted in artwork using spiritual models as subjects. I also perceive it as a showering of fine energy, arching and moving like the aurora borealis with an electromagnetic force that is ever changing, growing, retracting, adding hues of pink, green, and blue to create a rainbow effect.

From this point the soul line becomes more distilled to enter the physical realm. A vortex not unlike a sieve collects the universal energy of Creator and Creation, drop-by-drop, descending down a column of light. Like manna or a beautiful raindrop collected upon one's tongue, the soul line is clear, crystal energy becoming manifest into the physical condition. It is DNA forming in each cell and, in the larger perspective, the forming of a column of blue-white light.

A single strand of soul line looks like a strand of DNA, unwoven and spread out; combined, the myriad soul filaments form a column of vibratory light. "All cells in the world contain DNA—be they animal, vegetable, or bacterial-and they are all filled with salt water, in which the concentration of salt is similar to that of the worldwide ocean" (Narby 1988, 88). How inspiring that the word for soul arises from the German and Goth word *siawalia* (belonging to) the sea. The soul language of Euro-origin and biology would appear to be parallel or arise from a greater wisdom consciousness. Jeremy Narby goes on to say:

> DNA bathes in water, which in turn plays a crucial role in establishing the double helix shape. As DNA's four bases (adenine, guanine, cytosine, and thymine) are insoluble in water, they tuck themselves into the center of the molecule where they associate in pairs to form the rungs of the ladder; then they twist up into a spiraled stack to avoid contact with the surrounding water molecules. DNA's twisted ladder shape is a direct consequence of the cells' watery environment. DNA goes together with water, just like mythical serpents do" (Narby 1988, 88).

The soul line or hara has been captured in cellular drawings made by indigenous shamans who have trance journeyed into the physical molecular structure of the body seeking connection with the soul and who have traveled into the spirit realms upon these lines to bring back emotional and spiritual healing (Narby 1988, see illustrations 79-79, 81-85, 87, 89, 92).

The symbolic spiral or ladder of the soul line looks very much like a twisting spiraling rope in the energy field. It is constantly moving in a luminous state. I began seeing this phenomenon in childhood when I would "see into someone" but did not discover meanings for the beautiful shimmering blue-white structure until years later when I began studying energy medicine. When filaments or lines of the larger soul rope become traumatized, soul loss occurs. A fragment of the "soulular" consciousness disengages from the primary soul line and dangles out in space. When dismemberment happens, numbing out and all the attendant symptoms of soul loss begin. It is not until the soul fragment is caught and rewoven back into the primary soul line that soul recovery and integration can take place.

The rope-like structure I have observed has been described by the Ashaninca tribe of the Amazon as the "sky rope" (Narby 1988, 94). Many shamans have reported in their trance stories about following the rope ladder to find healing for the patient in the spirit world.

In Australia, Tibet, Nepal, Ancient Egypt, Africa, North and South America, the symbolism of the rope, like that of the ladder, necessarily implies communication between sky and earth. It is by means of a rope or a ladder (as, too, by a vine, a bridge, a chain of arrows, etc.) that the gods descend to earth and men go up to the sky...the shamanic ladder is the earliest version of the idea of an axis mundi (of the world) which connects the different levels of the cosmos, and is found in numerous creation myths in the form of a tree (Narby 1988, 63)

Some of the drawings that survive today of the DNA-like soul line symbol date to early Egypt, Taoist China, and the Aborigines of Australia who can trace their ancestry back 40,000 years (Narby

1988, 79). The striking symbol of the double helix is depicted as the double-headed serpent in many indigenous cultures.

> The theme of twin creator beings of celestial origin was extremely common in South America, and indeed throughout the world... the Aztecs' plumed serpent, Quetzacoatl, who symbolizes the 'sacred energy of life,' and his twin brother, Tezeatlipoca, both of whom are children of the cosmic serpent, Coatlicue (Narby 1988, 62).

The relationship between DNA in the physical body and the energy field soul line is that both are encoded with the soul's blueprint. That these two forms resemble one another so closely is profound. It is possible that shamans the world over have long been working with healing the soul (as depicted by soul healings illustrated on ancient petroglyphs, cave paintings, and carvings on wood and stone), and that biology has finally caught up on the scientific front. In this way ancient healing wisdom traditions meet in the 21st Century with science.

The blueprint of the soul is held in the soul line. Life's challenges and healing lessons are encoded within the shamanic practice of soul recovery which has been a practice of shamans handed down for millennia. In our post-modern world fraught with soul loss, the practice must be carefully and insightfully reintroduced as a psycho-spiritual healing way to come into balance and harmony on many levels. Sandra Ingerman's, Patricia Whitebuffalo's, and Kay Cordell Whitaker's views on this subject (see Chapter 3) relate directly to this teaching and healing way.

When soul loss occurs, the soul line I perceive appears to have a disconnected strand or strands hanging out in space. When I travel in trance states, I begin at home on the soul song of my patient, and I perceive where there are dark spots of departure. The spirit of my patient will show me where to look, and my ally spirits will take me out on the soul line of my patient. Any dark or fractured spot in the soul line is an indicator in trance state that soul loss has happened. I begin by holding the patient's hand, touching into the patient's soul line, and then tracking out into the spirit realms.

Soul loss depends upon the depth of the trauma, and the person's life lessons or blueprint. However, larger soul loss can also be tracked on levels involving a community, a country, or even globally. We can witness the soul loss in the Oklahoma City bombing case or in the Columbine School massacre, and in the terrorist attacks that killed thousands in our nation most recently. If we extrapolate soul loss into the arena of wars, famine and disease (such as AIDS in Africa) and sites of deprivation to our environment, we can, in concentric circles, track and find states of trauma existing globally. In these larger, more archetypal cases, soul loss is definitely evident. The tear in the fabric of the emotional bodies is evident. Deep rents delve even more deeply into the soul line of both individuals and nations. Being interconnected to all life, how could these causes not show up?

In the energy field there is an anchor of the soul line in the physical realm located at the high heart (also known as the thymus). Four chambers of light vibrate like a diamond or a star in the thymus region. From the high heart, the soul line weaves its way deeply into the physical world. Just like the beloved serpent, the One becomes one with the individual being, anchoring into the belly of the physical world. The soul line anchors into the lower abdomen—the home of personal existence and personal power in a spot about three inches on the midline directly under the umbilical cord in the abdomen. The soul line connects through the umbilicus into grounded nature—this present physical life. Drawing together this weaving from the vast webbing of all life, the soul line then continues downward through the body to connect with the deep core of creation, our Mother the earth. Anchored into the crystalline core, the soul line becomes a frequency highway of creation happening all the time. This weaving comes home to earth and a connection is made, an endless wave of creation. In that moment a star is born deep within each being—a consciousness that knows itself to be far greater than personality or species. It is the divine that exists within each sentient being. The final nesting doll, Creation/Creator (or any other name one may choose) exists in every sentient being at the very core of all existence. The fire of creativity constantly burns. There is no separation between God and Being. All is NOW. This essence is a renewable, unending source of fire that has been forgotten because of disconnection; and thus, we come to dismemberment, dissolution and forgetting—the condition of soul loss which is caused by separation.

Soul loss appears as a disturbance in the energy field which relates to specific life events that caused the condition. In the multidimensional energy system, the threads or filaments of a torn soul can be tracked from one dimension to another. Beginning with a client's history, there may be a very specific awareness by the client as to moments when fragmentation happened. For example, I have noticed in sexual and addiction abuse cases that awareness arises out of having lost "self."

Gathering the history of a person's life has always been an act of sacredness for me as a practitioner. Learning to hold sacred space and presence in listening to clients has been one of the major learning and "being" experiences of my life. I imagine myself as Spider Woman sitting with my client in the center of the universe. Then I watch and listen as the webbing of this soul's life is shown to me through their language and sharing trust, through witnessing and being present. It is a holy act and for me a tremendous privilege to enter into the client's universe. It is an act of complete yielding of my personality to listen to the language and to the song of another human being's life. I not only become the "witness" but also the "questioner" at specific moments; and also the "presencer" to keep us anchored in the NOW. Sometimes when we speak about our history, we believe that story to be running us now. The more identified we become with "story," the greater the concretization of the soul loss. Sometimes the story itself becomes the reason for existence with endless recycling and no apparent conscious movement toward shift or change.

Listening underneath to what is being said—listening into the silences is an art form, a way of being present and open to the truth. Language is sound carrying resonance, information, the soul's song, history, texture and feeling-tone qualities. Breath and silence between spoken language is even more filled with the mystery. I refer back into my body as my Divine Compass to feel how my body, its cells and "soulular" consciousness are resonating as the client speaks. I track the footprints of history, sound, and life of the client as I track into other dimensions and feel my way into all the sensate possibilities. This process is inner work married with the present outer world of what is being spoken. It is the first stage of contacting the soul's longing and the soul's blueprint. "Presencing" the client to these sensate experiences can be a healing experience on its own. Sensory awareness gets in under the radar screen of the ego and the mind..

"Being with the other," soul-meeting-soul, is a way of meeting the Beloved. I am often reminded of The Little Prince in his quest for truth when he reaches the moment in his journey where he meets the fox who shares his secret. "It's quite simple," says the fox to the Little Prince, "One sees clearly only with the heart. Anything essential is invisible to the eyes" (De Saint-Exupery 1943, 63). Sacred listening or "being with" is an expression of extraordinary love. It is in these moments, when the true heart sings the song of the soul and is met beloved-to-beloved, all potential opens. Everything is possible when seeing with the heart.

The soul opens like a beautiful lotus blossom reaching for the essence of the sun. The soul and the expression of unification the soul embodies in the heart-of-hearts has never been isolated or separated. But sometimes we forget all of this and need to be reminded of our true essence. Sometimes we live in another dream and need to remember ourselves. Life experience and traumas layer over the soul's song until it cannot be felt. When this happens, we are ready for "dismemberment." Soul loss experiences become our greatest teachers in finding our way back home—home to self, to our soul's life purpose, and to the greater I AM presence.

Soul retrieval as a specific healing ceremony is described by Kay Cordell Whitaker and Patricia Whitebuffalo from the shamanic perspective and by Judith Schmidt in "soul journeying" [Schmidt's term] in their interviews. The power of recalling the soul into the remembered state requires a foundation of trust, compassion and a sense of wonder on behalf of the client and practitioner. Imagination and intuition, experienced through the activation of senses (including the sense of spirit), unthaws the lost soul aspect and invites the soul to come home. Once this transmission has been completed, the next phase of healing arises. This is the act of conscious integration within the client's life.

Taking time and space to incorporate the soul in its fullness in the present is a creative process and is just as important as the healing ceremony. I paint pictures, write, make poetry, get new power songs from spirit, dance, plant flowers, and spend reflective time in nature. This way of integration is also how I advise clients to assimilate the healing. One of my clients recently brought me a quilt she is stitching based upon the images and energies she experienced as a result of her soul remembering. Her blanket has become a healing quilt. In this creative way, she is embodying the return of her soul memories. It is a beautiful work of art to witness.

I feel we do not spend enough time being sacred and reflective with ourselves. We seem so intent upon pushing forward into the next event in our lives. Integration time whether it is practiced through inner silence and meditation or actively, creatively manifested or both, is essential to reweaving the webbing of our life. It is in deep silence that spaciousness opens within us. In silence and space we can attend to the voice of our soul's wisdom arising. I experience the integration process in the soul line as a strengthening. The soul line becomes brighter in the energy field as the resonance of increased life force is rewoven. I witness the webbing of the soul line as it reorganizes and becomes coherent. Sometimes I hear what I have come to term "the celestial choir singing," as I bear witness to the soul's return. I feel this may actually be the soul's song I'm hearing. The key to transformation comes from within. Sometimes words do not describe the change or shift happening in the inner landscape. There is simply a sense of completion and wholeness that the soul is embodied consciously. This moment is a very sacred moment because healing is taking place on a "soulular" and cellular level.

Over the years, I have come to understand the soul's journey as having "challenge-teachers" and "ally-teachers." Challenge-teachers appear in life as hurdles, traumas, loss, grief—in short, as dismemberment or dissolving experiences which define moments in our web of life. Most recently as a nation we have encountered the loss of thousands of human lives through the acts of terrorism on September 11, 2001; or, as I feel it, the "911 wake-up call." My suffering through sudden and unexplainable deaths has been one of many "challenge-teachers" in my life. I sustained soul loss and fragmentation at the sudden death of my sister and husband only months apart. Post-traumatic shock enveloped me for years as I struggled to come back from the land of the dead. Having endured broken-heartedness and healing through soul remembering, I empathize with the families and pray for them and their dead. We are a people united in this tragedy as we were united in the Oklahoma City bombing tragedy. All of us at some level have been deeply affected. Shock is a "challenge-teacher." So is fear. It is a wake-up call and a tremendous call for remembering our true soul. "Challenge-teachers" can be generators of shock. To achieve balance, we must turn deeply inward to explore the nature of our help and support.

Coming together in family and community to share spiritual practices is part of our natural, organic grief process. Grief work is the work of the soul and is essential for the soul's growth. We must not sweep loss under the carpet. We are a nation needing to teach one another, through our grief, how to live in and from the heart. In this way we will call those shocked, split aspects of ourselves home.

To pretend "business as usual" as we have heard from the politicians in the name of keeping the economy moving is pure denial. The facts are simple, plain and very apparent. We are a nation of people who have not grieved openly. The community that developed after the Oklahoma City bombing is an "ally-teacher" for us. So is the community that came together after the Columbine School massacre. These communities recovered through the grieving process together. They provide us with soul remembering models. In the true sense of tribe, we must continually find ways back to remembering the true nature of our essence. This is a time of the heart cracking wide open. This is not a moment to "get over" in our culture. It is a time to delve deeply, become curious, ask questions, and explore the nature of our support. In short, it is a moment to remember our true nature, our ancestral soul and to bring healing to the forefront of our consciousness as we weave our lives back home.

What has been lost? What aspect of us is requesting to come home? How can we invite and encourage ourselves to become whole in the present moment? What places in our lives need reparation, reconciliation and unity? Where do we need to forgive and be forgiven? The soul recovery process requires deep inner work and self reflection. Transformation arises out of dismemberment. The heart cracked wide open becomes available for inspiration to enter in. The energy field naturally begins the process of soul reweaving and integration. With tools such as imagination, creativity, and our willingness to have our hearts lead the way, we begin to find our way back home. We cannot do this deep work alone. We must support and bear witness for one another in community. Healing arises from love, compassion,understanding and,curiosity .

As we learn self-response-ablility, we open the capacity to heal the past, creating an unthought-unknown potential to access spaciousness in which we build a way to our future and the generations who stand upon our shoulders. We have incredible capacity, and we must remember this from the depths of our ancestral bones. We have evolved before and we have the awareness to do so again. The question is really about choice, and awareness, and the really big one—taking action. It is true, as one soul grows—so do we all. What is your choice?

Chapter 5

Conclusion: Last Words

The Journey

Above the mountains
  the geese turn into
  the light again

painting their
  black silhouettes
  on an open sky.

Sometimes everything
  has to be
    enscribed across
    the heavens

so you can find
  the one line
    already written
    inside you.

Sometimes it takes
  a great sky
  to find that

small, bright
  and indescribable
    wedge of freedom
      in your own heart.

Sometimes with
  the bones of the black
    sticks left when the fire
    has gone out

someone has written
  something new
  in the ashes
  of your life

*You are not leaving
  you are arriving.*

(Whyte 1998, 37-8)

236

From the historical perspective, the fundamental causes of soul loss have not changed from the review of indigenous cultures in Chapter One. These causes are:

- severe fright
- shock
- terror
- anxiety
- accidents
- unconscious or conscious disconnection from and imbalance with nature,   the elements and the environment
- abhorrent and violent behaviors such as war
- death of a spirit guardian
- living out of balance with self and others

Symptoms of soul loss behavior are:

- conflicting behavior not normally part of a person's character
- memory loss
- the inability to focus and attend to life
- depression
- neurosis
- delusion
- dissociation
- increased separation from life
- stealing power
- disturbed sleep, restlessness
- anxious behavior
- addictions (all forms)

In our post-modern culture, we have added a very toxic cause: The intention to harm ourselves, others, and the Earth—our home. The reality of living in a mechanistic mindset increasingly creates more and more destructive patterns. As a human species, we are the most dangerous threat to the continuation of life on our planet. We are causing, through our continued insistence upon staying stuck in separation, a state of soul loss, which causes horrendous harm to all life. We have literally ripped out our cords of connection to the earth—the first three chakras. We continually dislocate our energy field, our feelings, our spiritual wisdom, our creativity and our imaginations. In short, we recycle the soul loss pattern creating negative complex scenarios and deeper and deeper states of separateness through disconnection. Each time we choose to stay disconnected from life, the pattern of soul loss becomes more entrenched.

Soul loss is being played out on a worldwide basis through violence, greed, control, misuse of power, manipulation and arrogance. In short, soul loss is a disease known as "victim consciousness." As a human species, we have added to the original causes of soul loss through the misuse of some technologies, sciences, and industries (i.e. nuclear power and nuclear waste disposal). We have done this in selective and consciously harmful ways.

> If you are run by your mind, although you have no choice you will suffer the consequences of your unconsciousness, and you will create further suffering. You will bear the burden of fear, conflict, problems and pain. The suffering thus created will eventually force you out of your unconscious state" (Tolle 1999, 190).

The soul loss state of victim consciousness is being used deliberately by some governments to overwhelm us and to keep us as a human species in a state of denial and worse, in a state of despair. In this loud state of soul loss, how can we hear the song of the earth? The soul song of the earth is also our song. Without our soul song, there is no possibility of reverberation to awaken, to change. Without our soul song, we have no vision for a balanced future. We become myopic, seeing only the monetary benefit of short term policies that keep us temporarily comfortable but reproduce the same self-destructive patterns. Humankind's short-sightedness has trivialized our "soulular" wisdom. We are in a moment whereby the suffering we are causing the world is the wake-up call! What tools, healing rites, and gifts do we have to awaken and to change? The capacity of our power to destroy is also the capacity of our power to create. How then, do we wake up our soul songs?

From my perspective, we can wake up by feeling, experiencing, and acknowledging the pain and suffering we are causing. Some of my students and clients say to me, "This is too overwhelming. It's too scary. What can I do as one person?" Fear and despair are symptoms of massive soul loss, yet they are the very keys to change. I feel we must be self-responsible for the reawakening of our creativity, imagination, and spirituality both as individuals and, in the larger context, in our being global citizens. Experiencing pain cracks the heart open. Pain is a major motivator in healing. Tolerating the discomfort and suffering we are causing ourselves and others is another key to awakening. Tolerating and exploring suffering allows defense, denial, and numbness to dissolve.

The first act of "soulular" recovery is to acknowledge what has been lost. Energetically, the cracked heart leads us to our soul song. When insight comes forth, a space opens within. Energetically, insight appears as a light shining in the darkness. Once insight is acknowledged, the grieving process for what is past has an opportunity for movement. We can also find a river of compassion and forgiveness in coming out of the frozen pattern of the past into the present moment. The symptoms of soul loss can be attended to by "being with" what has been lost. We can begin to track where our soul song is hidden and recover it by calling it forth. In calling our soul song forth, strength, clarity and energy returns. The more we reweave our soul song, the stronger our connection to all life becomes. We literally remember ourselves, and we can do this as individuals, as communities supporting one another, and within the larger context of remembering ourselves as citizens of the earth (and all cosmology).

When the soul song is strong, balance returns. Balance happens through taking action to correct and make reconciliation for the past. Balance is the reawakening of creativity, the imagination, and spirituality. Balance requires movement in order to change things. When insight arrives in any healing process, the danger is to say, aha! and leave it at that. What healing will come if there is no intention to change? I find in much of the New Age literature and thought a narcissistic tendency to believe that insight is transcendence. The belief is, once you have awakened, the spiritual job is done. In the process of believing that transcendence is the goal, the act of taking responsibility to clean up our mess is denied. Another New Age fallacy that is commonly bandied about is that our children will clean up our mess. We are it, folks! We are the ones who have put toxins in the earth. We are the ones who need to clean it up.

In reuniting with our soul song, we have an opportunity in the present moment to engage our gifts as a human species. Recycling old destructive patterns of our story causes soul loss. When the true essence of the soul is fully embodied, the past becomes powerless. In becoming soul-full, we can stop the spiral towards extinction. In *Medicine for the Earth*, Sandra Ingerman writes on the process of coming into balance. She terms it the "process of transmutation."

> ...intention + love + harmony + union + focus + concentration + imagination = transmutation. The invisible worlds and helping spirits do exist. By learning to communicate with these realms we can develop a creative partnership, bring the miracle of transmutation into reality...Know your divinity and shine your divine light..." (Ingerman 2001, 255-6).

We do not need to "fix" the earth. We need, through the process of becoming soul-full, to mend our relationship with the earth; and in so doing, to back track and clean-up our mistakes.

When I pray in the sacred Sweat Lodge, this is my prayer:

Grandmothers and grandfathers, Mother Father God, Creator and all creations hear these prayers.

To the southern direction, guardians and allies, spirit helpers and teachers of trust, love, and innocence, draw near and ground us so that our feet are planted firmly upon the Great Mother, our Earth. Teach us and show us the way so that we may live in right relationship with one another. And guide us each step in our earth walk so that our decisions are made from love. For the sake of the children, let us live in love.

To the western direction,
guardians and allies, spirit helpers and teachers of emotions, introspection, the unconscious, and other conscious realities, of thunder and lightning draw near and walk with us in the darkness so that we may grieve and face our shadows. Teach us and show us the way inward so we may face our destructiveness and in the dark find power in our suffering and strength in community. And guide us each step in our discomfort so that we do not turn away but live the good life for all beings; for the sake of the children.

To the northern direction,
guardians and allies, spirit helpers and teachers, ancestors and ancestral knowledge, clear our minds with the wind that blows away confusion and chaos. Teach us and show us the way so that we are cleansed and learn from our mistakes in a humble way. And guide us each step as we learn to forgive, reconcile, and remember our true inheritance; for the sake of the children.

To the eastern direction,
guardians and allies, spirit helpers and teachers, ignite our hearts with the fire of compassion and love. Inspire our imaginations so that we burn away what needs letting go and illuminate our vision. May we live in the power of our full song and
become
change makers here—now, for the sake of our children.

To the above direction,
Sky Father, Father Sun, Moon Mother and the Star Nations, guardians and allies, spirit helpers and teachers, guide us with your wisdom of the eons. Teach us and show us the way. Let us remember where we have come from in the Great Cosmos and our journey to this moment. Teach us to honor and respect all life; for the sake of our children.

To the center direction,
which grows the Tree of All Life, guardians and allies, spirit helpers and teachers, guide us in our soul's journey in the lessons we are here to learn. Help us to understand and to grow seeds of compassion for the sake of our children.

To the sacred, human heart within each of us,
we make a vow to 'walk our talk' no matter what obstacles are in front of us. We make this vow for the sake of the children who are here with us now, and for the unborn children yet to come.

We pray these words are heard and that we receive your compassion, help, and understanding. We pray that our words become our life, and that we live the Blessing Way.

We thank our ancestors for showing us the way home. May we continue to remember for the sake of those yet to come.

In every good ceremony of healing, there is an intention spoken at the beginning, prayer and sacred healing in the middle, and a vow to live the ceremony now. But the ending of ceremony is part of the circle of life—it never ends. The vow keeps on being as we keep on being. We can choose to forget our vows or we can live them.

Calling ourselves back home out of the state of soul loss into the state of soul remembrance requires help, support, guidance, community, love, creativity, willingness, yielding, dissolving, compassion, forgiveness, reconciliation, and generosity of spirit (although not in any particular order). These states are our "ally-teachers" and models. Any one of these soul-full states can open the portal into deep, true and lasting change. The same sequence can be pointed to in understanding the nature of suffering and pain when the "soulular" decision arises to change. These are our "challenge-teachers." It all distills down to choice—to live in love or to live in fear (and not to miss any steps along the way). We must experience our deepest fear in order to call ourselves home just as we must experience and embody the vulnerability of living in deep love.

In closing, I ask these questions: Where, how, and in what manner do you choose to live love and with whom? From the state of being soul-full: What can you say "Yes!" to living in balanced relationship with all life? What are your inspired visions for a world in balance? What is your commitment in making balance happen? How will you begin to live this, now?

I leave you with the words of the Heart Talkers, our elders and teachers. Their voices and their lives are models for living in a soul-full way. These living elders are our allies upon the journey home. Listen, once again, to their voices of inspiration which remind us of our divine and true essence and our humanity.

Kay Cordell Whitaker

The most vital, the most important thing, we can do for our children is to learn the truth of who we are as individuals, each of us, and live it, own it, show it, be it.

Don Alberto Tazto

The loss of the soul happens sometimes because of very strong fear. You could also lose your soul because the path you walk was not in harmony with you...It could also be because the person is very weak, maybe they don't have the right way of life, not a good way of life ...

Luisah Teish

I am trained at how to take a look…and how to rebalance the energies to get you back on track. That is what our rituals are about, getting you back in alignment with your sacred self and with nature, community and spirit.

Patricia Whitebuffalo

My challenge was not to allow my personal pain and loss of my ancestors to interfere with the healing. It's difficult, when we are living in our toxic debris, to make a major shift of consciousness. The lifting and clearing of that debris... would allow a global shift in consciousness.

Anita Barrows

I think the union model, especially, is a way home. What I look at with my adult patients and some of the adolescents is dreams. The dream is a manifestation of the soul; the dream comes from a place that we can't determine, and we can't control. The dream tells us things we sometimes don't remember, things that we don't necessarily think about in our conscious lives. Through looking at dreams, people really do begin to change at very deep levels and reach into something inside themselves that they have lost.

The other thing that I really encourage them to do is to take a look at the natural world, to offer back to nature, no matter how wounded they are. I think offering back is always a way of coming back to yourself.

Matthew Fox

Rollo May said, 'Myth is the foundation of values and ethics,' Remember that a myth is not untruth. It is a truth too big for a mere factoid, too big for a mere bumper sticker. The three myths governing this school (The University of Creation Spirituality) are as follows:

By changing work we can change history. The key to transformation is the transformation of work.

Cosmology matters. It gives us a context by which to understand our place in time and space...

Creativity matters. Creativity is the only thing our species really has going for it. ...It encourages us to recover our sense of co-creation with the Divine Creative Spirit that both 'hovered over the waters at the beginning of creation and hovers over the mind of the first artist at work.' (Aquinas)

Sandra Ingerman

The real question is, 'What is it that I really came into this lifetime to do?' What would really be healing in our culture right now is for people to switch their priorities around.

Focus on what is a good vision for our present and our future. We have so much creative potential. Especially after we get back that lost essence and vitality from the soul retrieval.

Arielle Guttman

...astrology is something that is a really valuable healing tool...Is there healing needed and where is it? ...What's going on underneath? My work has also been with the soul at a different level, through the charts. Is this person living the kind of life that his soul wishes him to be living? ... Every soul's chart has a certain moment in time when you were born and every moment in time is good for something. Every moment in time creates something...every moment equates to a song, a musical note, something in the universe, a cosmic resonance. It says, aha!, this is how you live in harmony with the moment you were born.

Sam Beeler

Our seven central beliefs are: 1) Honor the Creator; 2) All life is sacred and has spirit. 3) We are all equal; 4) Walk in balance with all creation; 5) The Earth is our Mother; 6) Honor the elders; 7) Honor the children.

Harmony is when you are in-sync with the internal and external environment. Balance is your place in the scheme of harmony. One must strive to be centered.

Judith Schmidt

Most often in the telling, there is a re-telling of a very old story, a story that is in a rut that causes suffering.

Fantasy is an escape from reality, a withdrawal from reality. It is an abortive attempt to enter what imagery leads one to, but it doesn't go there. In imagery...you will go through a dark space to get to a new space. In fantasy, you bypass dark places and you make yourself feel better by repeatedly going to a place that feels good...The intention of imaginal journeying is to journey, to discover, to open possibilities. The sensuous is a doorway to the mystical...If you enter through the senses, you connect with what infuses the senses.

We, as a species, are in a call to action. Our task is to remember our true potential as a species that has the potential to heal. Soul recovery is a responsibility every "two-legged animal" is being called to now. It starts with you and me remembering. Listen, once again, to the words of Don Alberto: *Shammu, Shammu, Shammu* (Come, come, come home). Let us sing the soul song, our own song, the song of the earth, and the song of the universe. We are part of the webbing of all life. When I experience the power of the word "universe," I see *uni* (one) and *verse* (song). We are one song.

Remember, remember, remember.

List of References

Achterberg, Jeanne. 1985. *Imagery in Healing: Shamanism and Modern Medicine.* New Science Library, Shambhala.

Barks, Coleman. 2001. *Rumi: The Glance Songs of Soul Meeting.* New York: Viking Penquin.

Berry, Thomas. 1988. *The Dream of the Earth.* San Francisco: Sierra Club Books.

Blackburn, Thomas C. (ed.). 1977. *Flowers of the Wind: Papers on Ritual, Myth and Symbolism in California and the Southwest.* Socorro, New Mexico: Ballena Press.

Davis, Wade. 1996. *One River: Explorations and Discoveries in the Amazon Rain Forest.* New York City: Touchstone Books/Simon and Schuster.

De Saint-Exupery, Antoine. 1943. *Le Petite Prince (The Little Prince).* Trans. by Richard Howard. New York: Harvest Book division of Harcourt, Inc.

Eisenberg, D.M. et al. 1998. "Trends in alternative medicine use in the United States: 1997. Results of a follow-up national survey. *JAMA.* 280: 1569-75.

Eliade, Mircea. 1964. *Shamanism: Archaic Techniques of Ecstasy.* Translated by Willard R. Trask. Princeton, New Jersey: Princeton University Press.

Elizondo, Virgil. 1998. *Guadalupe: Mother of the New Creation.* Maryknoll, New York: Orbis Books.

Fox, Matthew. 1979. *A Spirituality Named Compassion.* San Francisco: Harper.

_____. 1988. *Coming of the Cosmic Christ.* San Francisco: Harper.

_____. 1991. *Creation Spirituality: Liberating Gifts for the People's of the Earth.* San Francisco: Harper.

_____. 1999. *Sins of the Spirit, Blessings of the Flesh: Lessons for Transforming Evil in Soul and Society.* New York City: Three Rivers Press.

Hultkrantz, Ake. 1953. *Conceptions of the Soul Among North American Indians.* Stockholm: Ethnographical Museum of Sweden.

_____. 1987. *Native Religions of North America.* San Francisco: Harper and Row.

_____. 1967. *Religions of the American Indians.* Berkeley: University of California Press.

_____. 1992. *Shamanic Healing and Ritual Drama: Health and Medicine in Native North American Religious Traditions.* New York: Crossroads.

Ingerman, Sandra. 2000. *Medicine for the Earth: How to Transform Personal and Environmental Toxins.* New York City: Three Rivers Press.

Landy, David. 1977. *Culture, Disease and Healing: Studies in Medical Anthropology.* New York City: Macmillan Publishing Co., Inc.

Lawlor, Robert. 1991. *Voices of the First Day: Awakening in the Aboriginal Dreamtime.* Rochester, Vermont: Inner Traditions.

Lewis, I.M. 1971. *Ecstatic Religion: An Anthropological Study of Spirit Possession and Shamanism.* Harmondsworth, UK: Penguin.

Lyon, William S. 1998. *Encyclopedia of Native American Healing.* New York City: W.W. Norton & Co.

Macy, Joanna and Molly Brown. 1991. *World as Lover, World as Self.* Berkeley: Parallax Press.

_____. 1998. *Coming Back to Life: Practices to Reconnect Our Lives, Our World.* Gabriola Island, British Columbia, Canada: New Society Publishers.

Merkur, Daniel. 1983. "Breath-Soul and Wind Owner: The Many and the One in Inuit Religion." *American Indian Quarterly* 7(3):23-29.

Mooney, James (ed by Frans M. Olbrechts). 1932. *The Swimmer Manuscript: Cherokee Sacred Formulas and Medicinal Prescriptions.* Bureau of American Ethnology, Bulletin 99.

Napaljarri, Peggy and Lee Cataldi. 1994. *Yimikirli: Warlpiri Dreamings and History.* Melborne: Harper Collins.

Narby, Jeremy. 1998. *The Cosmic Serpent: DNA and the Origins of Knowledge.* Putnam, New York: Jeremy F. Tarcher.

Nawakadj, Nganjmirra. 1997. *Kunwinjku Spirit.* Melbourne, Australia: The Miegunyah Press/Melbourne University Press.

New World Dictionary of American English. 1988. 3rd Edition.

Nicholson, Shirley (com.). 1987. *Shamanism: An Expanded View of Reality.* Wheaton, Illinois: The Theosophical Publishing House.

Reis, Patricia. 1995. *Through the Goddess.* New York City: Continuum Publishing Company.

Rodriguez, Germán. 1992. *La faz oculta de la medicina andina.* Trans. by Charlene Wilson Bradley (2001). Quito, Ecuador: El Núcleo de América Ecuatorial.

Roberts, Elizabeth J. and Elias L. Amidon (eds.). 1991. *Earth Prayers from Around the World: 365 Prayers, Poems, and Invocations for Honoring the Earth.* San Francisco: Harper.

Robertson, Robbie, and the Red Road Ensemble. 1994. *The Native Americans.* "Twisted Hair," song from CD. New York: Capitol Records, Inc.

Ross, Rupert. 1996. *Returning to the Teachings: Exploring Aboriginal Justice.* Toronto: Penguin Books.

Ruiz, Don Miguel. 1997. *The Four Agreements: A Toltec Wisdom Book.* San Rafael: Amber-Allen Publishing.

Sarangerel. 2000. *Riding Windhorses: A Journey into the Heart of Mongolian Shamanism.* Rochester, Vermont: Destiny Books.

Stolzman, William. 1989. *The Pipe and Christ.* Chamberlain, SD: Tipi Press.

Suzuki, David and Peter Knudtson. 1993. *Wisdom of the Elders: Sacred Native Stories of Nature*, New York: Bantam Books.

Tolle, Eckhart. 1999. *The Power of Now: A Guide to Spiritual Enlightenment.* Novato, California: New World Library.

Villoldo, Alberto. 2000. *Shaman, Healer, Sage.* New York: Harmony Books.

Whyte, David. 1998. *The House of Belonging.* Langley, Washington: Many Rivers Press.

Wilson, Terry P. and Robert A. Black (eds.). 1983. *The American Indian Quarterly: Journal of American Indian Studies. Vol VII Num 3.* Berkeley: University of California.

Wolf, Fred Alan. 1991. *The Eagle's Quest: A Physicist's Search for Truth in the Heart of the Shamanic World.* New York: Summit Books.

Appendix A:
Biographies of Interview Subjects

Anita Barrows, Ph.D.

Anita Barrows is a poet, translator, and clinical child psychologist with a specialty in the treatment and evaluation of children with neuro-developmental disabilities and sexual abuse and is an Adjunct Professor at the Wright Institute, Berkeley. She is the author of articles on Ecopsychological Approaches to Child Development and Asperger's Syndrome and is active in the development of inter-disciplinary studies of psychology and ecology. She has earned various degrees at institutions of higher learning, including a Ph.D. from The Wright Institute.

Publications:

The Road Past the View
Rilke's Book of Hours
Review of *Turning the Wheel,* Barbara Green's film about a Tibetan community
Translator of Rainer Maria Rilke's *Stundenbuch*
Translator of Reed's *A Version of the Five Buddhist Precepts*

Contact Information:

The University of Creation Spirituality,
2141 Broadway, Oakland, CA 94612
(510) 835-4827

Matthew Fox, Ph.D.

Matthew Fox, a postmodern theologian, has been an ordained priest since 1967. He holds Masters degrees in philosophy and theology from Aquinas Institute and a Doctorate in spirituality from the Institut Catholique de Paris. Mr. Fox is president of the

University of Creation Spirituality and co-director of the Naropa Oakland MLA in Oakland, California. In addition to his work as a writer and teacher in the San Francisco Bay Area, he is a worldwide lecturer bringing the message of ecological and social justice, mysticism and blessing. He has received numerous awards and honorary degrees for his work in spirituality.

Publications (among 24 in total):

Original Blessing
A Spirituality Named Compassion
Passion for Creation: The Earth-Honoring Spirituality of Meister Eckhart
The Reinvention of Work
Sins of the Spirit, Blessings of the Flesh
Natural
One River, Many Wells

Contact Information:

The University of Creation Spirituality,
2141 Broadway, Oakland, CA 94612
(510) 835-4827, ext. 11
www.creationspirituality.com

Arielle Guttman

Arielle Guttman has been an astrologer for twenty-five years. She has also studied psychology and esoteric and spiritual astrology. Her work with personal teachers, all of whom are masters of their profession, helped her to synthesize and deepen her own astrological skills (Jim Lewis, Robert Hand and Alan Oken). Arielle has recently focused her attention on mythological astrology in which she combines her love of myth and archetypes with astrology. A second interest lies in the field of relocation astrology (frequently called Astro*Carto*Graphy® pioneered by the late Jim Lewis).

Publications:

Mythic Astrology (co-authored with Kenneth Johnson) 1993
The Astro*Carto*Graphy Book of Maps (co-authored with Jim Lewis) 1989

Contact Information:

Astro Originals, P.O. Box 31116, Santa Fe, NM 87594
(505) 984-8330
www.arielle.com

Sandra Ingerman

Sandra Ingerman is widely recognized for bridging ancient cross-cultural healing methods into the present and has been successful at interpreting them to meet the needs of the present time.   She is a leading practitioner of soul retrieval and is the educational director of The Foundation for Shamanic Studies. Sandra has a master's in counseling psychology from the California Institute of Integral Studies and teaches workshops on shamanism worldwide. Sandra is a licensed marriage and family therapist and professional mental health counselor in New Mexico.

Publications:

Soul Retrieval: Mending the Fragmented Self
Welcome Home
Following Your Soul's Journey Home
A Fall to Grace
Medicine for the Earth: How to Transform Personal and Environmental Toxins

Contact information:

Sandra Ingerman, P.O. Box 4757, Santa Fe, NM 87502
www.shamanicvisions.com/ingerman.html

Judith Schmidt, Ph.D.

Judith Schmidt is a licensed clinical psychologist who practices in New York and teaches nationally. The cornerstone of her work is the use of dreams and imagery as doorways to healing. She works with trauma, illness and the releasing of blocks to creative living. Judith also specializes in object relations, body awareness, and movement in her work toward unifying mind, body and spirit. Judith is co-founder of the Center for Intentional Living, a training and growth center for integrative psychotherapy.

Publications:

How to Cope with Grief

Contact Information:

Judith Schmidt, Ph.D., 26 Boulder Lane,
Goldens Bridge, NY 10526
(914) 232-7370
jschmruach@aol.com

Luisah L. Teish, Ph.D.

Luisah Teish is a writer, storyteller and spiritual guidance counselor. She is an initiated elder in the Ifa/Orisha tradition of the West African Diaspora; holds a chieftancy title from the Fatunmise Compound in Ile Ife, Nigeria; and chairs the World Orisha Congress Committee on Women's Issues. Ms. Teish was awarded a Ph.D. in Spiritual Therapeutics from Open International

University's School of Complementary Medicine in Colombo Sri Lanka. She has studied indigenous Native North and South American traditions (including the Caribbean). Further she holds workshops, lectures worldwide, and holds faculty positions at various colleges and universities.

Publications:

Jambalaya: The Natural Woman's Book of Personal Charms and Practical Rituals
Jump Up: Good Times Throughout the Seasons with Celebrations from Around the World

Contact Information:

Luisah Teish, University of Creation Spirituality, 2141 Broadway, Oakland, CA 94612
(510) 835-4827
www.ibukole5@aol.com

Don Alberto Tazto

Don Alberto Tazto is a Master Yachag Birdperson residing in the High Andes Mountains. He is a teacher and healer of the Cotopaxi Quecha tribe in Ecuador and a powerful Andean shaman strongly influenced by spiritual teachings of the east. In 1992 the Dalai Lama and numerous Tibetan lamas visited with Andean Yachags and elders (including Don Alberto) in Ecuador and Peru, passing over to them the spiritual responsibility of the planet. Don Alberto gives workshops, lectures, and performs ceremony in the U.S. and in Ecuador. He takes on apprentices who live and study with him for extended periods in Ecuador.

Contact Information:

www.donalberto.org for information about Don Alberto and upcoming workshops.

You may reach his U.S. assistant, Silvia Reynoso, at
www.summer@seqnet.net

Patricia Whitebuffalo

Patricia Whitebuffalo, teacher and therapist, combines her natural shamanic gifts, and her deep connection to the Earth, with her professional training. She is a graduate of the Barbara Brennan School of Healing, The Core Energetics Institute, and The Center for Intentional Living. She also maintains a private practice and facilitates workshops internationally. At present she is in the process of completing her first book entitled, *Wheel of Awakening,* which incorporates the ancient wisdom of the Medicine Wheel and the process of psychological/spiritual transformation.

Contact Information:

(831) 457-4056
pwb@cruzio.com

Kay Cordell Whitaker, Ph.D.

Kay Cordell Whitaker is a teller of medicine stories, a seer, healer and a "Thrower of the Bones," one of the world's oldest methods of divination. Kay undertook a highly unorthodox thirteen-year plus apprenticeship with two Native shamans of the Eastern Andes whose teachings included traditional psychology, storytelling, shamanic medical training and spiritual practices of the indigenous peoples of eastern Peru. In addition, she studied for more than five years with the lineage carrier of the mysteries of the Berber tribes of Africa. Her workshops focus on healing ourselves and our planet, and finding equitable solutions to daily problems. Kay is a graduate of the University of California at Santa Cruz and the University of Oregon where she also taught for several years.

Publications

The Reluctant Shaman – A Woman's First Encounter with the Unseen Spirits of the Earth Sacred Link – Joining Fortunes with the Unknown

Audio CDs by Kay Cordell Whitaker:

Song Magic
Dance of the Earth Fire Serpent
Power Animal Journey
Drumming to Journey By
Amazon Drumming to Journey By
Soul Retrieval Journey – Mending Your True Self

Contact Information:

A World In Balance, 7 Avenida Vista Grande #323, Santa Fe, NM 87508-9199
Phone: 505-466-3387; Toll Free: 866-335-4109
E-mail: song@worldbalance.com
Website: www.worldbalance.com

Sam Beeler, Ph. D.
Bird Clan, Keetoowah

Sam Beeler, Ph. D. is Bird Clan, Keetoowah of the Sand Hill Band of Indians in New Jersey. From 1970-1977 he was the Director of the New Jersey Indian Center; 1977- 1998, Director of the Paumanok Algonquain Foundation; 1998 to present, Director of the New Jersey Indian Office; and is Chairman and Keetoowah Council Member since 1988.
Dr. Beeler sits on the Permanent Forum for Indigenous People at the United Nations and serves on the Committee for Human Rights.

Contact Information:
Dr. Sam Beeler
New Jersey Indian Office
955 River Street Station
Paterson, N.J. 07544-0955

Visit: www.sandhillindians.com
or contact Dr. Beeler directly at
beeler@CherokeeNation.zzn.com

About the Author

Jane Ely, Ph.D., D.Min. is trained in transpersonal psychology, imaginal therapy, journey work and energy medicine for transformational healing. She most recently earned her Doctor of Ministry from The University of Creation Spirituality, founded by Matt Fox. In addition, she follows the spiritual traditions of her American Indian elders and is an enrolled Cherokee and Mi'kmaq. She is also a storyteller with a CD entitled Ancestral Journey. She teaches internationally on the subjects of ecopsychology emphasising our inter-relatedness with all life; dream work; peacemaking skills; and healing practices with a focus on returning to sacred ceremony. Jane is the Dean of The Peacemaker School of Spiritual Healing, www.peacemakerschool.com. She lives in Hawaii where she can be reached by email: deerclan2@verizon.net

About the Author

Jane Ely, Ph.D., D.Min. is trained in transpersonal psychology, imaginal therapy, journey work and energy medicine for transformational healing. She most recently earned her Doctor of Ministry from The University of Creation Spirituality, founded by Matt Fox. In addition, she follows the spiritual traditions of her American Indian elders and is an enrolled Cherokee and Mi'kmaq. She is also a storyteller with a CD entitled Ancestral Journey. She teaches internationally on the subjects of ecopsychology emphasising our inter-relatedness with all life; dream work; peacemaking skills; and healing practices with a focus on returning to sacred ceremony. Jane is the Dean of The Peacemaker School of Spiritual Healing, www.peacemakerschool.com. She lives in Hawaii where she can be reached by email: deerclan2@verizon.net

Printed in the United Kingdom by
Lightning Source UK Ltd., Milton Keynes
137935UK00001B/239/A